"I loved reading '363 Days'. Whereas this is not a dramatic front line war story, the author intimately shares his very personal and unique experiences that touched my heart and opened my eyes a little wider."
John M. / California

"The author was able to bring the reader into his writing, one almost felt like they were also reliving his time in Nam. I highly recommend this book, especially for those of us who lived through that era. This is a fresh perspective."
Judy F. / California

"Highly Recommend this book. (The author) did bring back a lot of the same feelings many of us had during our time in country."
Allen Y. / Illinois

"I genuinely enjoyed this book and I feel that it adds something important to the Vietnam War narrative. This memoir tells of a common man's experience in nearly a year of supporting the American role in Vietnam. It's clear and concise and adds an important voice to the mix."
Emily B. / California

"I thoroughly enjoyed reading this book. Having never been in the service, the author brought me in to the experiences of the day to day existence of a young man fighting an unpopular war. The story is mostly about the "behind the lines" experience but you never know when the behind the lines becomes the front line. I would highly recommend this book to either someone of that generation or younger."
Bill S. / California

"This book is the real deal, written so well by the author that you could actually feel the monsoons, the heat, and the glory of a Thanksgiving dinner. It is an honest perspective on being a G.I. and growing up fast."
Paula L. / Illinois

COPYRIGHT

363 DAYS IN VIETNAM

A MEMOIR OF HOWITZERS, HOOK-UPS & SCREW-UPS FROM MY TOUR OF DUTY 1968 TO 1969

MICHAEL STUART BASKIN

THE COVERS

FRONT:

The author, Spec 4 Michael Stuart Baskin shortly after target practice on LZ Buff, day 362 of his tour of duty.

BACK:

The author, Spec 4 Michael Stuart Baskin leaning on a 105MM howitzer, at Fat City around day 150.

INDEX

To my dad

Donald Stuart Baskin

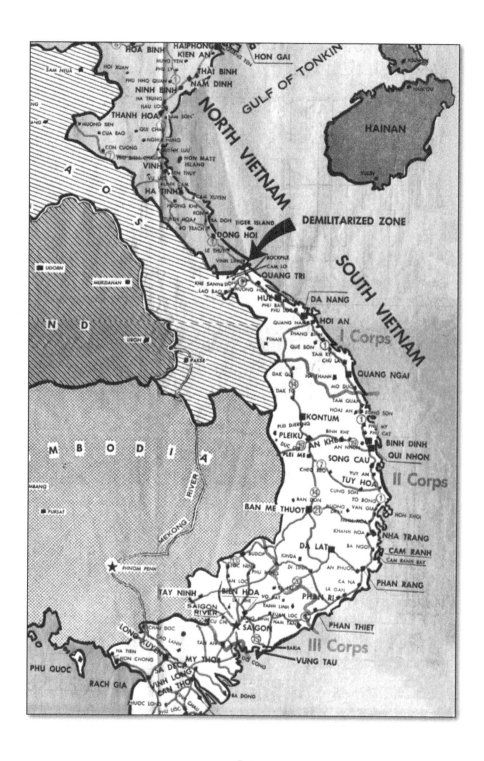

BRIEFING

Most of what the average person knows about the Vietnam War is gleaned from movies, TV dramas and documentaries like the one Ken Burns' produced in 2018. Almost every one of those (even the documentary to an extent) revolves around the infantry: their horrific combat, courageous heroes and historic battles.

What everybody doesn't know is that for every infantryman, there were between 6-7 soldiers working to *support* the infantry in a myriad of ways. Put another way, less than 20% of the guys in Vietnam were in the infantry. The +80% of us that weren't 'grunts' have ALL kinds of stories to tell even if they're not 'war' stories, per se.

Since getting back from Vietnam, I've occasionally shared my experiences (orally) with interested friends and acquaintances. Subsequently, a number of them asked why more vets aren't willing to talk about their experiences in Vietnam.

Over the years I've given that question some thought and here's what I think . . .

It's possible the vet feels like his stories might not live up to the heroic expectations his *audience* might have. If a soldier was a mechanic or cook or electrician or had one of the scores of non-combat jobs, he might not think he had a story worth telling 'cause it was just a 'job' - a job that wouldn't be very much different (except for the heat, humidity, bugs, snakes, exposure to disease and various, constant threats of death) in any other place.

He may have done regrettable stuff - participated in or witnessed atrocities. Or the guy may have been unheroic in a life-threatening situation. Unless you were there, there's no possibility you could understand the reasons for the decision(s) guys in those situations made and there's no way to predict who's going to hold someone in contempt over what they did or didn't do.

Maybe the vet killed in self-defense but hasn't come to grips with the moral or emotional consequences. Even if a person killed out of self-preservation, beliefs might condition him to feel guilt. And what would the reactions of others be if you told them?

What if the vet suffers from PTSD? A vet probably isn't going to share much if he's haunted by nightmares.

What if the vet had participated in some kind of retribution against one of *our* guys?! Or what if he had fathered or 'might have fathered' a child while there? Or something else? Only that vet knows - the ghost of regret wears a thousand faces.

All Vietnam vets as well as their peers grew up hearing about WWII from their parents, TV shows, TV documentaries and the movies. We all knew only too well how heroically our side had answered the call and subsequently won. The Vietnam vet's story could **never** favorably compare to the justifiable heroics of WWII.

Even though we may have won every battle in Vietnam, ultimately, the war was **lost**. For a vet to tell his story, he has to tell it in spite of the military failure even if it wasn't *our* failure.

Let's not forget how unpopular the war was or how little fanfare accompanied the vets' return after serving. Some of us even had to endure criticism for our participation!

Last but not least, a vet may not be all that verbal - he may not know how to tell his story – he may not be a good storyteller or writer.

It could be a combination of some or all of the above.

I wasn't dissuaded.

When I considered writing my recollections of Vietnam, I didn't know where it would lead – 50 years had past before I got inspired to record those experiences. How many stories did I have/how many could I remember? How well could I tell them? And, of course, would anybody care?

Regardless, I launched into it and like a line of dominoes, one story after the other seemed to fall from my memory onto the page.

I've tried to keep the prose real without being vulgar. Some events involve themes that include sex, drugs and gore. It gets very personal, somewhat controversial and, at times, there's no way to avoid how gruesome it was.

Some (friends) would suggest simply omitting potentially offensive events. I haven't done that. It would reduce my story to a histrionic, year-long sleepover in Vietnam. Censoring those parts would make the story not worth telling.

This is what I experienced - it's complete and it's true. Nothing is added, nothing is invented.

My story may seem unusual, but there were tens of thousands of non-infantry, Vietnam vets who confronted similar situations, challenges, screw-ups and disasters. Every G.I. having *boots on the ground* in Vietnam during the war would have stories like these. When added to the existing narrative, I believe these stories help to complete the picture of what happened during those tragic times.

Spec 4 Baskin at home before leaving for Vietnam.

JULY 13, 1968: DAY 1

. . . I landed in Vietnam. No, it wasn't a Friday.

My immediate impression was, 'I'm going to have to get used to this heat' which, luckily, I eventually did.

At the 'In Country' orientation I couldn't not be distracted by these 2-foot long lizards darting in and out of holes on the side of a bull-dozed dirt berm 30 feet from where I was seated . . . over and over again. They'd scurry out of one and into another - it seemed surreal and totally appropriate.

Then somebody passed out duty assignments and loaded most of us on a Chinook helicopter - the first of dozens of chopper flights - the only way to get anywhere in Vietnam.

I don't think I was issued my M16 - everyone's constant companion - until I got to my artillery battery in Chu Lai. We didn't visit the mess hall, take a shower or sleep without having our M16 nearby. I didn't keep a round in the chamber, but the 20-round clip was always inserted and always full.

The dress code *in the field* was somewhat relaxed - shirts were optional. Mustaches were okay but had to be neatly trimmed. All buttons and insignia's were embroidered with black thread - shiny objects on one's shirt were visible from long range by snipers. All the clothing issued to us was OLIVE DRAB GREEN - the socks, undershirts, handkerchiefs and boxer shorts.

I was 10,000 miles from home, surrounded by an invisible enemy sworn to kill me if he got the chance and total stranger-comrades whose implicit priorities were to stay away from danger and keep themselves safe above all else. It wasn't 'every man for himself', but it felt like it to this new arrival.

I was disoriented and anxious. If there had been a *cause* worth fighting for, it might have been different, but there wasn't. The thought of spending the next 364 days in this primitive, dangerous country was overwhelming – like being in a tunnel without a flashlight.

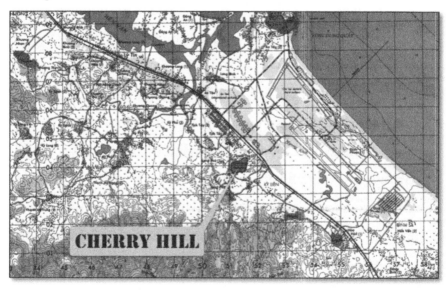

A topographical map with my first duty station
Cherry Hill across the road from the airport in Chu Lai.

DAY 3

I was assigned to the headquarters detachment of the 16th Artillery in the 3rd Battalion, Americal Division stationed at a base called 'Cherry Hill' just southwest of the Chu Lai Marine Air Base. It was a fortuitous post – 1. It wasn't infantry and 2. It was located in the northern sector of the country, but well south of the DMZ and a couple miles from the South China Sea. The weather was pretty agreeable compared to down south and inland - think sand dunes instead of jungles.

There was a LOT of us G.I.'s surrounding and defending the airfield and Cherry Hill felt safe even at night though that could have been a mistaken impression. One of the take-aways from my tour in

Vietnam was the false sense of security one felt during the frequent, prolonged non-combat intervals.

My military training/job ('quartermaster/small arms specialist') vexed the commanding officer – they already had a 'supply sergeant' in charge of requisitioning supplies, all the men maintained their own weapons (M16's mostly) and I'd never seen a howitzer in person before. They didn't have a second slot in the organizational chart for my position and they were probably looking to transfer me to some other outfit from day one.

The supply sergeant (let's call him 'Bob') made me his 'man Friday' while I was assigned to the 3rd of the 16th and did his best to keep me busy, but nobody made an effort to get to know me. Bob told me the whole unit had been U.S. National Guard in Nebraska until an act of Congress 'activated' it and send it to 'Nam. I felt a bit like an outsider, but didn't realize until later that my discomfort was also because I was the 'temporary' new guy.

DAY 9

I don't remember very much from this period – maybe because I didn't have a routine job and maybe because I was still in a daze to be in Vietnam. I remember feeling adrift - lost.

I was eating three meals a day, so the mess hall was a big part of everyday. As you undoubtedly imagine, Army food was not *haute cuisine* – instant scrambled eggs or S.O.S. in the morning, various cold-cut sandwiches for lunch and water buffalo/beef with potatoes and a vegetable for dinner. Actually, the all but tasteless, tough meat of the water buffalo may have been served in some form or another at every meal – it was a common source of food for everyone in Vietnam.

The 3/16th Artillery at Cherry Hill ate its meals in a shared mess hall - a long, reddish-brown, wooden building that housed a dinning area and kitchen. At mealtime, there would always be a line to get in – there were more G.I.'s than places to sit. Before we got the nod to come in, we'd stack our M16's against the wall outside – no rifles were allowed inside.

While waiting to get in I noticed Vietnamese civilians going through the trashcans just outside the entry. That struck me as very odd. For starters, this Midwestern suburbanite had never seen a person so down on their luck they would stoop to scavenge discarded food out of the trash. Furthermore, they were doing it in full view of dozens of us.

Secondly, it seemed contradictory to the instruction I had just received at the 'in country' orientation. Didn't they warn us about the possibility of ANY Vietnamese person, male or female, being Viet Cong or a Communist sympathizer? Not only was this Vietnamese guy on our base, he was picking through our trash!

How desperate does one have to be to eat food out of the trash? Isn't that the kind of person who would favor regime change? How hard would it be for him to leave a bomb in the trash? How hard would it have been for him to grab one of our loaded M16's and shoot the place up?

I was so disoriented at the time, I just figured this was the status quo here, kept quiet and minded my own business regardless of how uncomfortable the trash scroungers made me feel.

3rd Battalion   16th Artillery

DAY 16

While some baby boomers may have traveled outside U.S. borders by age 21, I had not. Until Vietnam, the most unusual place this Chicagoan ever experienced was Florida. My expectations of what I'd see in Vietnam were limited to TV newsreels which usually focused on battle scenes, not the daily life of the Vietnamese people. And yet, part of me expected most of what it turned out to be like.

I love to travel now, but not Vietnam in 1968. G.I.s had been strongly cautioned to avoid unfamiliar places – for me that pretty much meant the whole country. We were discouraged with stories of smiling shopkeepers who spiked Cokes with battery acid and glass shards, concealed bombs in souvenirs and pimped prostitutes with sharp objects in their genitals. Any Vietnamese person could be a Vietcong sympathizer. Then there was the routine booby-trapping of the major thoroughfares. Yeah, you could say it spooked me - I kept my travel 'in country' to the minimum.

Nevertheless, some travel within Vietnam was inevitable. Driving the short distance from Cherry Hill to the PX in Chu Lai gave me a brief, stark glimpse into the land and its culture. The abject poverty and ubiquitous destruction stunned me. I formed an indelible impression of the country as well as its inhabitants.

I wish I had a better camera and had taken more photos, but at least my fledgling journalistic instincts got me these polaroids taken from a moving jeep.

A bombed out residence or temple.

DAY 21

My first military mission was to accompany Sergeant Bob on a 'search and capture'. Our battalion commander (a Lieutenant Colonel) wasn't happy with the folding, wood-framed cot Uncle Sam had provided. He directed us to find and procure an inner spring mattress and steel frame so that he could sleep better. Sergeant Bob knew just where to look.

At daybreak (or maybe after breakfast) we set out for the Naval base a couple miles away.

The base was somewhat shocking - it felt like we weren't in Vietnam anymore. The buildings looked like they had been flown over from the States! They were so much better built than the crude, sandbag-covered bunkers and wood-frame hootches us Army guys had. There were even sidewalks and some landscaping. It was a different world.

We entered one of the buildings and there was a *Navy* bed, waiting in the entry for us - it had a six-inch thick mattress on a steel frame with crisscrossed steel wire support.

After some obligatory small talk, Sergeant Bob disappeared, presumably to work out the deal. Visions of TV's Ernie Bilko bartering for a case of beer flashed through my mind.

When he returned, we quickly loaded the bed on our ¾-ton utility vehicle and we were off. Mission accomplished.

I didn't get to see the Lt. Colonel's reaction, but he must have been pleased - it was quite the upgrade.

Now, I don't know what naval rank a G.I. needed to qualify for this *luxurious* bedding in a combat zone, but I'm pretty sure a seaman didn't have to be a Lt. Colonel and DIDN'T have to trade a case of Jameson. For the sake of comparison you should know that 'Lt. Colonel' is two ranks below General.

So all you mothers out there take note: don't let your sons grow up to join the Army - the Navy has the best beds.

Bombed bridge on the way from Cherry Hill
to Chu Lai Naval Station.

DAY 25

I'm encountering a number of Vietnamese men and women on our base, Cherry Hill and outside the Chu Lai Post Exchange (PX) and they're not what I expected – at least they don't act like I would have thought.

The Post Exchange in Chu Lai.

We, the U.S. military have traveled halfway around the world at a cost of billions of U.S. taxpayer dollars and we're engaged in a life and death struggle to save *their* country from being overrun by the Communists in the north. Naturally, I expected them to display a tone of some gratitude and appreciation.

Despite our commitment and sacrifice they treat us/me with a surly indifference – even when they're guests on our military base, Cherry Hill. As I walk by they yell out, "Hey G.I. you want buy some (trinket)? You want buy some 'P' (Piasters - Vietnamese currency)?"

Me: "No thanks."

Them: "You numba 10 G.I. You numba 10! You numba 10 fucking million!"

Me: "Huh?"

Them: "Oh, just kidding. You numba one, G.I. Yeah, numba One . . . one fucking million. Ha, ha."

So I'm thinking, 'maybe it's just that guy or those two guys' or her, but no, almost every Vietnamese person I meet has the same attitude, the same chip on his/her shoulder. They act like they did NOT want us here.

Am I missing something? There's something very wrong with this picture – I don't get it. Don't they understand Americans are dying to protect Vietnamese independence? Don't they understand:

WE DON'T WANT TO BE HERE?!

Don't they understand:

It's gonna get WORSE if we leave?!

DAY 34

According to Commanding General, Westmoreland, to ultimately win THE WAR, we G.I.'s first needed to win the *hearts and minds* of the South Vietnamese people. So the commanding officer of the 3rd of the 16th Artillery thought he would do *his* part by providing material support for an orphanage in Quang Ngai. Naturally, he delegated the actual work to Sergeant Bob who organized a convoy to hand deliver medical supplies and some toys.

Sergeant Bob had a job for me, too: gunner on the lead jeep.

I don't remember thinking I had any choice in the matter and besides, it sounded kind of adventurous. Famous last thoughts.

Quang Ngai was maybe 40 miles south of LZ Cherry Hill. The route was infamous Highway 1, which was routinely mined overnight by Charlie. What us worry?

Our jeep was equipped with an M60 machine gun mounted in the jeep's middle, behind the front seats. The convoy consisted of only 3 or 4 vehicles.

It was a beautiful, sunny day. Highway 1 had more potholes than any road I'd ever been on and we took it slow – 25 MPH or less. I wore my helmet and flak jacket and kept one hand on the M60 to keep it from flopping around.

Up to that point I had never fired a machine gun on 'full automatic' and was itching to fire the M60. I negotiated with Sergeant Bob to *test* the gun. At some point when we seemed to be in the middle of nowhere, he motioned to stop and pointed in the direction I should fire. It worked just fine.

Quang Ngai was more than a village but not quite a city. The orphanage had two stories, some big trees and lots of kids. My job was to mind the vehicle while most of the other guys delivered the goods.

Once the mission was accomplished we were off towards Cherry Hill. At some point I remember the driver getting impatient with the pace and speeding up.

Almost immediately, the cotter-pin holding the M60 on the mount gave out while I was holding the gun with both hands. In the blink of an eye, me and it were airborne. Both of us landed on the gravel road hard. I remember thinking I'm going to get run over, but the driver of the deuce and half (truck) behind us saw everything and stopped in time.

One hand and forearm and one knee were scraped and my brand-new birthday watch had a smashed crystal, but I was fine. Sergeant Bob and the driver instantly ran to my aid and were extremely apologetic. I was shaken but slightly embarrassed by all the fuss.   (continued)

The driver took it slower and I cradled the M60 like Schwarzenegger in 'Terminator' for the remainder of the trip.

The side of Highway One between
Cherry Hill and Quang Ngai.

DAY 41

Despite the brevity (though it didn't feel brief at the time) of my *career* in the U.S. Army, I experienced a few military 'game-changers'. The most significant was probably our (the U.S.) first modern involvement fighting a guerrilla foe. Another was the ubiquitous use of helicopters for transportation and firepower. Let's not forget the first use of computers.

The biggest change I experienced first-hand was the M16.

Through the first 7 weeks of basic training, we were issued M14's – an 'old school' rifle. It was much longer and quite a bit heavier than the M16. It was merely semi-automatic and used a clip that only held about 10 rounds. It had a wood stock and I thought it resembled rifles deer-hunters used.

Everything about the M14's size was awkward. The length meant it was always shifting around on your shoulder while marching and needed to be adjusted for comfort constantly - the weight hurt your shoulder after less than an hour. Crawling through the mud with it was very difficult. The live-fire course was a disaster due to its awkwardness. I felt like I would have been a dead man if that had been real combat.

All Army recruits in March '68 were required to 'qualify' on the shooting range with the M14.

During the last week of basic training, we were introduced to the M16. Impressive! It was shorter, lighter, had a 20-round clip, a hollow, plastic stock and a switch that converted it to FULL AUTOMATIC. I immediately felt like this was the weapon of the future.

On the firing range the M16 was fine for the closer targets but not well-suited to the 600-yard ones like the M14 had been. I qualified as 'expert', but always wondered if the bar had been lowered - I wasn't at all confident past the 300-yard targets.

At the Quartermaster school (after basic training), we spent all our time learning to service the M16 (as well as the other common small arms in use in Vietnam), but no time with the M14.

In Vietnam I never saw anything but M16's (M60's, M79's, .45 pistols and .50 machine guns). M16's had already been in use there and I wondered why we didn't train with them from day one.

DAY 46

Experienced my first B52 strike today. It was so far away in the hills over the western horizon we didn't see anything, just heard the deep rumble of dozens of big bombs exploding in very quick succession. Never saw or heard the plane(s), either – they dropped their payload from high altitude.

I didn't keep track, but I must have witnessed thirty B52 strikes. They got to be common and sometimes we didn't even look around to see where the strike had been unless it passed a certain loudness threshold.

About half the time they were close enough to see the dense, smoke from the blasts, but if the target had been past the horizon, we'd just hear the rumble.

Every time I flew over Vietnam I was struck by how many craters pock-marked the landscape – they were literally everywhere. It was amazing to think how many bombs and rounds of artillery had been fired and left their marks on the countryside.

DAY 49

From time to time Cherry Hill's mess hall served as a movie theater. They threw up a temporary screen at one end of the room and served free popcorn. There was only one 35MM projector so there would be a delay in the action every time the reel needed to be changed, but we didn't mind – it was much better than no movie at all.

Usually the movie was an old classic I had already seen, but tonight's show was a brand new flick: 'The Green Berets' starring John Wayne. It was kind of weird - that movie was about the war in Vietnam.

Wayne's movies were predictable – prior to the opening credits you could be pretty sure it would portray us G.I.'s as the good guys and that we would prevail against evil Charlie's overwhelming odds by movie's end. Furthermore, you could anticipate a feel-good ending and a boost in the morale for us troops watching it.

That's exactly how it played and despite the accurate prediction, my morale was somewhat better when it was over. I guess I'm a sucker for those 'Hollywood Endings'.

DAY 55

It's said that God moves in mysterious ways – well, so does the U.S. Pentagon, at least so far as my experience suggests.

The U.S. Army went to no small expense training me for a specific job: Quartermaster and Armorer, yet, it would be a job I all but never fulfilled in my three-year enlistment. The Army never assigned me to an outfit in Vietnam or the U.S. or Germany (my three duty stations) that needed the specific skills they had spent 8 weeks intensively educating me to perform.

In '68 the Army may have been overwhelmed by its share of the newly authorized 55,000 draftees and enlistments every month. That adds up fast and it's a LOT of guys to administer. Under normal circumstances the powers that be would have maybe taken a moment to reflect on where this or that person's talents could best be utilized, but either there weren't enough hours in the day OR it really didn't matter.

Anyway, I'm speculating and getting ahead of my story . . .

While assigned to the 3/16th Artillery I was enjoying the cushy life (relatively speaking) of Chu Lai at Cherry Hill . . . eating three mess-hall cooked meals a day, benefitting from the relative security of its heavily-armed location and basking in its nearness to the ocean. On the other side of the ledger, I'm pulling more than my share of Kitchen Police and all-night guard duty and I'm sitting around with little or nothing to do everyday that isn't spent as a cook's personal slave.

So I propose to Sergeant Bob to take a company-wide inventory. I would account for every weapon and every bullet in the entire detachment. He likes the idea – mostly because it saves him from having to either invent something for me to do OR explain to the C.O. why I'm twiddling my thumbs.

To be continued . . .

Taken from a moving jeep on
Highway One near Chu Lai.

DAY 64

I shared the hootch I lived in with about six G.I.s. It was a rectangular, wooden-frame construction with a corrugated tin roof and wrap-around screened windows. The entry was at one end and there was an exit to a windowless, sand-bagged bunker on the other end.

I got back after a day of counting M16's and was about to kick back on my bunk when one of the other guys approached – a specialist I had met from the motor pool. He told me they had a Vietnamese woman back in the bunker who was screwing anyone for $10 and did I want 'in' (on the opportunity).

However horny I was, that didn't appeal to me – frankly, it repulsed me. I told him 'no', he gave me an 'are you sure' look and disappeared into the bunker.

My barracks mates looked at me differently and didn't seem as interested in talking to me after that. Oh, well, we didn't have a lot in common anyway.

DAY 71

The Inventory of small arms and ammo in my detachment of the 3/16th Artillery: one bullet, two bullets, three bullets, etc. Boring stuff. Even recounting the anecdotes of unauthorized weapons that turned up, the curt refusal of the C.O. to have his guns included and my gushing over the .50 machine gun in the guard tower can't prevent that story from inciting yawns.

Around the same time the Armed Forces Network was playing a song that haunted me: 'Those Were The Days' by an unknown songstress, Mary Hopkin. The lyrics and tone were saturated with sadness. At 21, I didn't have a past to regret, really. Nevertheless, the song's melancholy possessed me and will forever provoke memories of a place I would have given anything not to be.

DAY 76

No sooner had I finished the inventory of small arms and ammo for the 3/16th than I was transferred to an artillery battery in a different outfit (!) – Delta battery in the 1st Battalion of the 14th Artillery. I got my papers, was told to pack my things and away I went in less time than you can say," Slam, bam, that's 'THANKS' in Vi-et-Nam!" I don't think Sergeant Bob even said, 'Good-bye'. I never saw any of the guys I had just met from the 3/16th again despite relocating to the 1/14th side of the same base, Cherry Hill.

I was picked up in a jeep by a G.I. of equal rank who was *supposed* to partner with me in the quartermaster duties for Delta Battery. I can't remember his name, but let's call him: 'Homer'. Homer was a 'good ol' boy who never looked me in the eye and never partnered with me in anything.

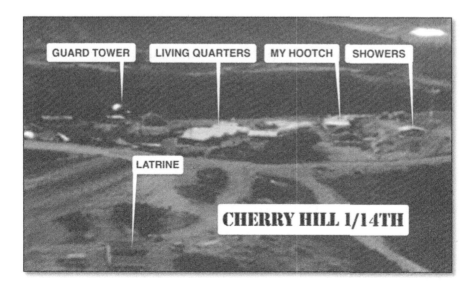

39

DAY 77

Delta Battery (Homer and me excepted) was at a different location - LZ Fat City about 4 miles northwest of Cherry Hill. We bunked side by side in a small frame shack with a corrugated, tin roof. We were the only two people in that shack. Ours was situated in a group of about a dozen identical shacks that all seemed to be similarly under-populated.

There was no one supervising us. Every day, Homer would disappear after breakfast. He never informed me where he was going or what he was doing. He never gave me any guidance as to what I was supposed to be doing or introduced me to any of the other G.I.'s in our unit. I had never met the 1st Sergeant or the executive officer or the commanding officer – no one. Homer was my only liaison with Delta Battery. I knew something was wrong with that picture, but I didn't know WHAT until later.

On the days I wasn't on KP (i.e. most of the time), I'd get up, eat, kill some time, eat, kill more time, take a shower and eat again. I read. I walked around the motor pool. I practiced guitar. I polished my boots and cleaned my M16. I made trips to the PX. I even visited the beach. It was weird, but it was easy and I was checking days off my tour of duty without breaking a sweat or getting shot at.

If I had any previous normal experience in the Army, I would have realized Homer was keeping me in the dark to preserve his cushy assignment. He had MY job and had figured out he could finish his time in Vietnam as the 'supply guy' as long as he could keep me from knowing anything or anybody. If I had known what my responsibilities were, I would have performed them more efficiently than Homer could imagine and he would have been reassigned to 'the field' with the rest of the artillerymen.

Delta Battery's Cherry Hill hootch.

DAY 88

Homer and I only occupy the west end of our framed hootch – the other 2/3rds is reserved for 'storage' (despite being empty most of the time) and occasionally a G.I. from Delta Battery sleeps in that section overnight prior to leaving for R&R or to return home after his tour of duty. On this night, Sergeant Tom stayed with us before flying to Bangkok.

Tom had just agreed to reenlist and was happy to share his reasons. In addition to receiving an automatic promotion from sergeant to staff sergeant (rank insignia: three up – one down), Tom was given a second R&R. The purpose of this second trip to Bangkok was to confirm his marriage to a girl he met there on the first trip.

While I was outwardly happy for him I couldn't help but see red flags. He told me they had met in a bar and produced a photo of her. Naturally, she was quite pretty and I couldn't help but wonder how many other G.I.'s had fallen in love with her.

Tom told me she had taken him to her parents' house for dinner and how nice they were and how they approved of her interest in him. He also told me they approved of her work as a prostitute which, he said, was an accepted job in Thailand and those red flags were suddenly everywhere.

I was dumbfounded. I just met this guy, he's on cloud nine over this woman and there's no way I can tell him what I'm thinking. So, I shake his hand, bid him 'bon voyage' and silently vow: 'I'm NOT going to make the mistake this guy's making!'

Sergeant Tom and his 105MM howitzer.

DAY 91

It's the autumn of 1968 in Vietnam. There's a war going on and the only thing I'm killing is time. Not that I want to be 'killing' anything, you understand - it's just that every day I wake up and wonder how I'm going to keep busy. Somewhere in the back of my mind I'm thinking 'why was I needed to be here?' but I tried to not let myself dwell on that.

Around the same time I met a guy who had a cool, non-operational control panel in his hootch – with all manner of dials and knobs - it was statically displayed on his footlocker, I think. I asked him where he got it and he told me about The Salvage Yard – the place military gear went when it was deemed 'out of date' or no longer useable even though it might still have uses. My inner scavenger was instantly piqued.

I borrowed a jeep from the motor pool and managed to find these burial grounds. The salvage yard was a wonderland of old military junk.

I combed through piles of random items – a LOT of it was just plain junk, but not all of it. There were stripped-down control boards from I-don't-know-what loaded with meters, rotary knobs and potentiometers which could be reused even though I didn't have a use in mind. There were numerous circuit boards stuffed with electronic components. There were gutted chassis of armored personnel carriers that could make excellent bomb/mortar shelters if buried. There was stuff I couldn't identify and didn't want . . . and there were large, heavy, canvas tent sections with sturdy wood poles. As I examined the tent parts, a light went 'on'.

My hootch had large, screened, window-like spaces between a knee-high wood base and the roof. These screened spaces extended completely around the hootch. The screened area was intended to catch cooling breezes. Since Vietnam rarely got much below 55 degrees and since we were ALL the same gender, privacy wasn't a thing and cooling was the priority.

The problem was rain. It rained frequently and if the wind was blowing, too, the inside of the hootch got soaked. The Army's solution was to cover the big, screened spaces of the hootches with sheets of thick, translucent plastic keeping both rain and cooling breezes out and making the hootch pretty uncomfortable whenever it got hot.

When I saw those tent parts in the salvage yard, I imagined: Awnings! Eureka!

I gathered enough materials for two awnings and headed back.

My awnings were simply designed - canvas cloth supported by a frame of tent poles. The cloth was secured at the top with a hem of nails and the poles were held in place by the weight of the cloth and friction. That allowed for the poles extending the awning to be collapsed if too much rain was getting in.

It rained, the awnings performed up to spec and I went back for materials to build more. When I had finished, not only did the hootch have cooling breezes and keep the rain out (without the sheets of plastic), but it looked snazzier than all the other hootches.

I was quite proud of my modification to the place and surely would have taken photos to commemorate it, if they had lasted longer.

To be continued . . .

DAY 94

It was mostly fun and games and KP duty until the monsoon arrived. I had just finished installing the four awnings around the west end of our hootch when it began.

During my 30-day leave prior to Vietnam, I did a little research about the country and I was expecting a monsoon even if I didn't know when. After three days of constant rain, I reckoned this was it.

I grew up in Chicago, so I'm no stranger to rain, but this was a downpour that didn't stop. It rained hard and then it rained harder. It rained all day and all night without so much as a slight let up.

I found out later that somebody in the Pentagon had figured 'rain' might be an effective weapon against Charlie and the U.S. was seeding the clouds to increase the amount of rain and slow him down. This strategy may have worked – in my time there, Charlie tended to be a fair weather foe.

Of course, the monsoon sword had two edges and the other edge made life miserable for our troops, especially the infantry. I cannot imagine how awful it must have been for guys living out of a tent in the boondocks. Those guys deserve our eternal gratitude for what they must have endured.

In the second week of October 1968, U.S. military meteorologists predicted two inches of rain for the Da Nang area just north of Chu Lai. To everybody's surprise, 36.7 inches fell THAT WEEK ALONE. And after a solid week of constant rain it wasn't over.

It was no picnic for me even if my only ventures outside were to the mess hall and the latrine. The Army's wet-weather solution for G.I.'s was a tent-like poncho. Ugh. It made normal activities difficult at best. It kept the hands free (sort of) but was constantly falling across your eyes and restricting your arm movements. Beyond that, your pant legs got soaked below the knee and it really wasn't compatible with our need to carry a rifle - I never did figure out a good way to carry my M16 when wearing the poncho.

The rain continued for two straight weeks – 14 days.

I listened to a lot of radio while hunkered down in my hootch – radio that reminded me of the life I was missing and seemed to focus on my misery. The Beatles had just issued single 'Hey Jude', which could have been about me. Hendrix covered Dylan's 'All Along the Watchtower' which also seemed to be about my situation. I've already mentioned, 'Those Were the Days' which HAD to be about me.

Yeah, I started to feel sorry for myself.

Cherry Hill during the monsoon taken from my hootch.

DAY 100

They say, 'Timing is everything' and mine seemed to be awful.

I had the misfortune of becoming disillusioned with college at the very moment the U.S. Congress created the Vietnam-era draft, sucking up 55,000 men each month. Rather than wait to be drafted, I enlisted to increase my chances of avoiding becoming an infantryman in Vietnam which obviously had partially backfired. Then I applied to Officers Candidate School, only to be denied because with so many guys available the bar had been raised to exclude anyone lacking a 4-year college degree.

I was sitting alone in my hootch reading Ian Fleming with the Vietnamese monsoon pouring rain outside when a G.I. acquaintance of an acquaintance opened the door and invited himself in. He was killing time, too and we shared some of our collective misery. When he was ready to leave, he held out his hand with a couple small red pills. "These will pick you up," he said.

Me: "What are they?"

Him: "A stimulant . . . 'methedrine'."

Me: "How do they make you feel?" Him: "Alive! Energetic. Here, they're free (as he put them in my hand)."

Him: "Take them in before dinner and you'll stay up all night - you'll have fun. Go to the club (the NCO club), meet people, it'll be great."

Then he was gone and I thought, 'what have I got to lose?'

Famous last words . . .

I took the pills and visited the NCO club like he suggested. At some point they kicked in and I found myself talking nonstop to a couple guys I didn't know at the bar. A lot of people do that every day, but not this introvert.

The bar closed and we were asked to leave at some point, but I was still buzzing. I slogged through the rain and mud back to my hootch – I don't remember Homer being there and made some attempt to entertain myself: reading, playing guitar, whatever.

At some point it wasn't fun anymore. I couldn't sleep. All I could think about was the rain and being 10,000 miles from home in Vietnam. I wasn't afraid – I was depressed and the more the drugs wore off, the more depressed I got.

By the time it started to get light outside, I was mired in self-pity and severely depressed.

DAY 101

I was beyond miserable – the worst I had ever felt in my life. I felt trapped with no way out. It seemed like the walls were closing in, like I was in a vice about to be crushed. I was panicking.

I visited somebody – probably the battery clerk - he suggested counseling. I agreed to see one – the clerk arranged it. A jeep showed up and drove me to see . . .

Frank. He was a probably no more than an intern psychologist from the Boston area. Nice guy. He quietly listened to me as I told him I desperately needed to go to the U.S. – that I just wasn't cut out to be here – *surely he understood that.* I don't think I told him about the methedrine. As I pleaded with him part of me thought: 'he doesn't have the authority to make that happen', but I pressed on.

When I finished, he smiled faintly and told me there was nothing he could do – that I would be fine and sent me away.

I slogged through the rain back to my hootch thinking all was lost, but the drugs were wearing off and I started to feel better.

Gradually I returned to normal. Maybe it would be okay and maybe it wouldn't, but it now seemed like the only way I would get out of here was to serve the time. I was stuck here and needed to make the best of it.

I resolved to never take methedrine or any stimulant like it for *recreation* again.

In hindsight, maybe that (experience) was a valuable lesson learned at minimal personal expense. And maybe my timing wasn't so bad after all.

Insignia for the 1st Battalion, 14th Artillery.

DAY 104

The monsoon ended. It was a sunny morning and *oddly*, both Homer and I were in the hootch when a couple officers I had never seen before strolled up and knocked on our door – a major and a 2nd Lieutenant with a clipboard. The tone of the junior officer's voice gave me a bad feeling as he asked if we would step outside.

We dropped whatever we were doing and hastened to comply.

The major cut straight to the chase as we stood at attention, "Who authorized these . . . awnings?"

Homer: "No one, sir."

The Major: "Do you see any other buildings with awnings, specialist?"

Homer: "No sir."

The Major: "The living quarters at Cherry Hill need to conform to the same standard, specialist. What if the guys in this hootch (pointing right) wanted to, let's say, build a skylight? And what if these guys over here (pointing again) wanted a swimming pool?' Can you imagine how disruptive that would be?"

I couldn't, but Homer responded: "Yes, sir."

The Major: "Take these awnings down, specialist. Now."

Homer: "Yes sir." Without hesitation, he spun around, grabbed the closest awning and yanked it as I stared in disbelief. After he pulled that one off, he went to the next as the Lieutenant looked at me: "Why are you standing there, specialist?"

I reluctantly assisted, repressing my anger, disappointment and embarrassment.

In a couple moments the four awnings were lying in a pile waiting to be returned to the Salvage Yard while our hootch once again looked as boring and plain as all the others (photo page 39).

At that point the Major turned and left. Before rejoining him, the Lieutenant instructed us to dispose of the 'garbage' and disappeared around the corner of our neighboring hootch.

I'm standing there stunned, confused, angry and wondering why these jerks lived with that broomstick up their ass and why did the Army have to be so STUPID.

I was so shocked and confused by the whole thing it wasn't until weeks later I wondered: did the Major think of this on his own or was he 'tipped off'? If so, who? Guys in a neighboring hootch? Or Homer?

DAY 107

A couple days after the 'awning' debacle (and my visit to the psychologist), I got orders to get my butt to Fat City – apparently my *creativity* coupled with an apparent *instability* meant I needed more supervision.

I didn't think much of it at the time – probably because I'd never met anyone as enigmatically deceitful as Homer, but it *must* have been him who put the burr under Major Tentpole-up-his-ass'es saddle. Furthermore, when he reported the awning incident to our CO, Homer undoubtedly added how useless I was in helping with the quartermaster chores. His plan to countdown the remainder of his days cocooned at cushy Cherry Hill would succeed. After I left Cherry Hill, I never saw him again.

My new assignment was still near Chu Lai about 4 miles northwest at an LZ named 'Fat City'.

Fat City was a different kind of base – the smell of gunpowder and diesel fuel permeated the compound. The frequent thunder of artillery punctuated the 'soundscape' and the *buildings* were mostly sandbag-covered bunkers. Fat City was an active 'fire base'.

Welcome to the war, Specialist Baskin.

Sharing the base were 155MM and 'self-propelled', 8-inch howitzer batteries, an armored cavalry company, the ubiquitous infantry and my unit, Delta Battery featuring six 105MM howitzers.

The name 'Fat City' was odd considering its care-free, 'life of Riley' connotation. Maybe, at the beginning it had enjoyed a more relaxed atmosphere, but that was then, before it became the scene of numerous round-the-clock combat missions.

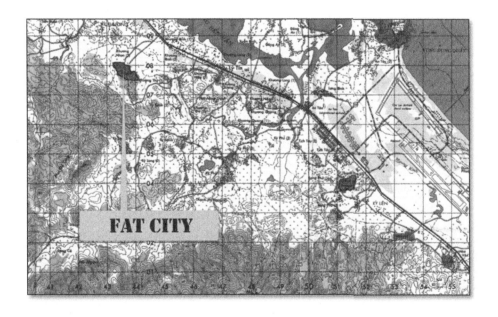

Fat City was fairly close to Cherry Hill, but oh so different.

DAY 108

One of the first orders of business at Fat City was a meeting with the commanding officer, Captain Alexander. He was a few years older than me and had graduated from West Point. My aversion to guys of his cadre was offset by his seemingly approachable personality and my respect for West Point grads – this guy had earned his rank and was *in it* as his profession, unlike the proverbial '12-week wonders' who attended the Army's 'Officer Candidate School'.

Captain Alexander remained seated, but looked me in the eye when he welcomed me to 'D' Battery and promised 'they would find something for me to do', which I understood to mean something other than what I had been trained for.

Apparently, they didn't know where I was going to fit in and rather than bunking me with just anybody, I was given a hootch all to myself – semi-solitary nonconfinement. It had a handy push-pin billboard/wall which I appropriated and in no time decorated to suit my likes.

Nothing too unusual about my choices: Hendrix, Cream and (my friend Chris Nielsen's) Mama's Bootleg Blues Band as well as Miss June and October. I enjoyed filling that big white space with stuff that motivated me to make it back alive.

Speaking of which, just about every G.I. marked days off a calendar – as you can see, mine was close to the center of attention.

The little collection of books underneath Miss June didn't really occupy much of my time, but I read Ian Flemming and random science fiction back then.

It's hard to make out, but the tent-like thing on the right side is the edge of a mosquito net over my cot. I don't remember needing one until I got to Fat City, but I was thankful to have it there.

Those squiggly lines running helter-skelter in the upper right? A Charlie-Brownesque strand of Christmas lights. Where and how I got them, only God remembers. Powering them up is another mystery – on firebases like ours, AC was a privilege generally reserved for officers. (continued on next page)

(continued from page 57)

Last but not least, see the seven, small nondescript cardboard containers located on the shelf to the left of the plastic washbasin? C-rations. They came in mighty handy after the mess tent closed. If you were hungry enough, they weren't too bad . . .

I hope you'll overlook the trance-like expression - when this photo was taken I'm probably thinking: 'what am I doing here?'

The Command bunker behind the 1/14th sign at Fat City.

DAY 109

The first day to go exploring my new base was gloomy, rainy and, believe-it-or-not quite chilly. No, not winter cold, but the dampness combined with temps in the 40's was surprisingly uncomfortable. We weren't really issued clothing to deal with this - I had on the three layers of clothing I was provided. I'm thinking: 'who knew it could be like this in Vietnam?'

And in the back of my mind I'm thinking: 'What else am I going to learn the hard way?'

This was my first chance to see howitzers in action up close and I have to admit: I thought it was kinda cool as long as I didn't think about the people that might be dying where the rounds were landing. The gear-head in me was fascinated watching those amazing machines and the coordinated teamwork that went into operating them.

Photos on the next two pages: #1 has 155MM howitzers. #2 is a self-propelled 8" howitzer #3 is an Armed Personnel Carrier & #4 is our quad-50 being tested. That's four .50 caliber machine guns mounted on the back of a 2½-ton truck - awesome firepower when used against enemy ground forces. Hiding behind a block wall would not shield you from that monster.

DAY 113

My new home at Fat City was about 100 feet from one of Delta Battery's 105MM gun emplacements. On this night a platoon of infantrymen must have been in some real trouble north of our position. That gun nearest me was south of my hootch and fired directly over me until about 3 AM. The guns were loud from any vantage point, but the shock wave is directional - they're about twice as loud when pointed in your direction.

Being relatively new to the artillery, I was fascinated and watched from the south side of my hootch for about a half-hour.

They fired a round every couple minutes. The other five guns were probably firing, too, but from my hootch, the only gun that mattered was the one 100 feet away firing over the top of the hootch.

At some point they stopped and I got to sleep for a couple hours.

DAY 119

This photo of me pointing a gun at the camera has a lot to tell.

A towel fastened around the waist with flip-flop footwear was NOT in the military dress code UNLESS the G.I. was in a warm combat zone and about to take or had just taken a shower. In this case it was the latter.

In 1968 there were zero women in combat in Vietnam or anywhere in the U.S. Military. Wearing only a towel was NOT provocative on a base exclusively staffed by men. In my one-year tour of duty I saw exactly 2 American women - they were Red

Cross gals and it also involved a shower, but that's another story for later . . .

You'll notice a five-gallon gas can to my left. Modern plumbing did not exist for the Army in Vietnam. I imagine - but don't really know - the Navy or Air Force may have had running water, but we never did.

When we wanted to shower, we needed to fill the can, carry it to the shower, carry the can up a ladder and pour it into the cut-off 55-gallon drum that sat above the shower. Five gallons would produce water for about 5 minutes.

If you wanted a shower that lasted more than 5 minutes, you could carry two five-gallon cans. I tried that once, but carrying two of those heavy cans exceeded my point of diminishing returns and I learned to 'make do' with one.

You'll also note that my M16 accompanied me 'cause Charlie, like Allen Funt, liked to show up when 'you least expected him'.

Despite the fact that any Vietnamese person could and sometimes did turn out to be Viet Cong or a sympathizer, there were a few Vietnamese civilians working on our base. One of those was a young woman who I had seen previously hanging around.

So, I've returned from a refreshing shower at the end of a workday, I've got the water can in my right hand and the M16 in the other. I'm looking forward to a delicious meal at the mess hall (haha) and as I approach my hootch, she casually walks right up to me and snatches the towel. She's looking me over and laughing as I snatch it back. Another G.I. had put her up to it.

I rewrap the towel around my waist and for reasons I don't remember think: 'this is a Fuji moment'. I ask if she'd take my photo. She's still laughing as I fetch the camera from the other side of that screen door. She's got a plastic flower in her hand and as I point the gun, she sticks it in the barrel (of the gun) like a stateside peacenik at a protest march. You can just make its pedals out.

Ordinarily, I would not point my rifle at someone. Ordinarily, I don't *carry* a rifle and ordinarily, the person I'm pointing it at wouldn't stick a plastic flower in the barrel, but there's nothing *ordinary* about this moment and you see the result.

DAY 122

On this peaceful, crystal clear night, I was gobsmacked by how easily I could see my way around our compound without the need of a flashlight. There was zero light pollution due to our being in the middle of nowhere and zero air pollution thanks to our quiet guns and location just west of the ocean. A full moon radiated off the whitish sand to create a dreamy, semi-lit landscape like none I'd ever experienced before or since. This may have been a hellhole, but on that occasion it was supernaturally gorgeous.

As I was walking by a bunker/hootch, I heard AFVN radio and conversation and stuck my head inside. There were about six guys sitting on the floor/ground – I had met one of them (Keith) who waved me in. The tight, candle-lit space smelled of incense and 'Nuoc Mau 100's'. The conversation paused when the AFVN DJ introduced the latest Cream album and it seemed as though I might have found a few kindred spirits.

My buoyant mood got leveled, though when the DJ announced Cream's disbanding and then followed with a performance of one of their new tracks featuring a 17-minute drum solo.

I felt genuinely betrayed. A. HOW COULD THEY QUIT AT THE PEAK OF THEIR CREATIVITY AND BEFORE I HAD SEEN THEM IN CONCERT? and B. (with the drum solo of 'Innagadadavida' fresh in mind) WHO IN THEIR RIGHT MIND WANTS TO LISTEN TO A 17-

MINUTE DRUM SOLO? By the end of the track, question 'B' was mostly answered, but there was still the fact there wouldn't be any more musical inspiration from Cream to look forward to. Damn, musically-gifted egotists!

At some point afterward somebody pulled out a guitar which got passed around. When it was my turn, I lead a few verses of the Beatles' 'Hide Your Love Away' followed by the oh-so-relevant 'Masters of War' by Dylan.

If every night could be like that, my tour of duty wasn't going to be so bad after all. But, of course, that wouldn't be the case.

DAY 124

One of our 105's was firing when I wandered by their pit in a moment of boredom and decided to watch this afternoon. The guy calling the shots (pun intended) was one of the guys passing the *peace pipe* in my visit to the *hangout* bunker a couple of nights ago: Sergeant (I'm pretty sure his name was) Don.

At some point Sergeant Don noticed me sitting there and I asked if I could pull the lanyard. He nodded and I may have pushed the other guy out of the way after leaping from my perch on the pit wall en route to the gun.

They were setting defensive targets at the time, not a real fire mission so amateurs were welcome to participate.

Defensive Targets, aka 'Delta Tango's' were typically set by infantry patrols (in the field) before it got dark so they'd be ready if Charlie tried to swoop in under the cover of darkness. They'd identify places where he'd be likely to hide and zero in on them while it was light. Then, if he did attack after dark, they'd simply call in 'Target Beta'. That target would already be dialed in and high explosives would be on the target in under 60 seconds.

Now I've got the lanyard in my grasp – I am pumped! Don makes eye contact and gives the command: "Fire." I am only too happy to comply.

B O O M !

THAT WAS FUN!

I'm not used to having *fun* here. I'm pretty sure that was the first *fun* I've had since getting here.

They make some adjustments, reload and Don gives the command again: "Fire."

Okay, I admit, I'm not thinking about the destruction this could cause – I'm thinking how cool it is to pull the trigger on this beast.

More adjustments and another BLAST!

A few more pulls and we're done – the targets are set and I've got a new way to pass the time in the afternoons. Hoo-Ahh!

DAY 129

If being stationed in Vietnam in November of 1968 was living a nightmare, pulling guard duty there made it worse and serving Kitchen Police (KP) there was the essence of 'cruel and unusual punishment'.

Well, guard duty wasn't terrible, but two hours 'on' and two hours 'off' (sleep) was completely unnatural. They didn't give you a day to prepare or a day to recover. I remember falling asleep once while standing/leaning on sandbags and barely catching myself before hitting the ground when my knees buckled.

On another occasion, an M79 grenade launcher was assigned to our guard bunker. The M79 kind of resembled a huge-caliber, sawed-off, single-barrel shotgun. It's ammo was a bit smaller than a grenade and was 'point-detonated' – i.e. exploded on contact. I had learned about servicing that gun in my advanced training, but had never gotten the chance to fire one, so you can probably guess what came next.

Via radio, I attempted to coax the officer of the guard to let me shoot it, but he didn't acquiesce until I told him I thought I saw movement on our perimeter. He wasn't fooled, but gave in, anyway.

Without any training on how to aim the thing – it's more like firing a mortar from the shoulder than a rifle – I overshot my target. I probably woke some G.I.'s up, but so what - it was a 'hoot'. Well, a 'boom' is more accurate. I asked for more practice shots and got a firm 'negatory on that' from the officer.

KP sucked. You had to be there by 4 AM and weren't done until maybe 10 PM.

The common image of KP is a 'sad sack G.I.' peeling a mountain of potatoes by hand and that was certainly among the usual chores – one of the nicer ones, actually. Cleaning stuff was what I hated, especially the greasy stuff and baked-on stuff. Cleaning that stuff was bad enough stateside with running water, big washtubs and well-lit facilities, but in Fat City we didn't have any of that.

The topper (and the thing I never understood) was the way the cooks (some of which I out-ranked) treated us - like we were their personal slaves. I never pulled KP with cooks who weren't verbally abusive.

The last KP in November of '68 was my turning point – I HAD to find an assignment that got me off that stinking duty roster and I had a plan: I would talk my way into the Fire Direction Center.

I had a positive experience in a similar situation as a kid. Our City League Baseball team had two pitchers – one was quite good and the other stunk up the place. The stinker happened to be the son of the coach. I KNEW I was better than him so I approached the coach one Saturday morning before the game and asked if I could have a chance to pitch. He immediately put me on the mound and after about 10 pitches, told me I was going to be the starting pitcher that day. Long story short, we won that game with me pitching all seven innings and I became the second starting pitcher on the team.

Working at FDC involved math and I knew I could handle anything up to and including trigonometry. The guys in FDC were exempt from all guard and KP duty due to their 12-hour, 7-days-a-week work shifts and if that's what it took to escape KP, then so be it.

One of Delta's 105MM's setting defensive targets at Fat City.

DAY 130

The morning after that last KP I marched up to the C.O.'s bunker - the door was open and I knocked on the doorframe. Captain Alexander was writing at his little, makeshift desk and looked up at me. "What is it, Baskin?"

"Sir, my talents aren't being utilized to their potential. I have the skills needed in FDC and that's where I could be of some good use."

He put his pen down. "Is that so? How is good is your math?"

"Very good, sir. I got 'A's' in Algebra, Geometry and Trigonometry."

"Huh. (pause) Okay, I'll look at your test scores (he meant the army entrance exam), talk to FDC and let you know."

"Thank you, sir." I don't remember having any doubt that I'd get in as I spun around and walked away. For one, I suspected he'd like me to be doing something, anything useful and for another, I had seen my test scores from that exam (the Armed Forces Qualification Test) – they seemed to be comparable to I.Q. scores and my 148 in math should be more than good enough. Furthermore, I'd met some of the guys in FDC – it wasn't staffed by Einsteins – anything they could compute, I could compute.

DAY 131

My confirmation to FDC took about as long as it takes to say 'a score of 148 in math.' It was a win for everybody, especially me - my first real assignment in Vietnam and, regardless of my previous training, ultimately my best, but that's getting ahead of the story...

I was placed on the 2 PM to 2 AM crew which meant I wouldn't be able to hang (in the evenings) with the guitar-playing buddies I had just met – I was sorry about that, but life is the choices you make and I had to get off the KP duty roster.

As it turned out, I was assigned to the FDC 'A' team. This was the crew that got the lion's share of combat fire missions and ALL the 'kills'. (According to 'VIETNAM STUDIES - FIELD ARTILLERY, 1954-1973' by Major General David Ewing Ott, 75% of the artillery combat fire missions occurred during the hours of my shift.)
You may have been wondering when or if 'kills' aka 'body count' was going to come up. Until now, I hadn't been involved with 'killing the enemy' – it was what was going on in the background and the implicit mission of the U.S. military, but I wasn't involved, even indirectly. After joining the FDC team, I was inevitably, unavoidably implicated as much as the guy setting the charge or loading the gun or pulling the lanyard – I became one of the guys responsible for each round hitting its target – the enemy, i.e. 'Charlie'.

I can't speak for other units, but Delta Battery didn't pick fights. In my experience, we merely helped to defend the infantry when they encountered trouble and needed support. And as far as that's concerned, I'm not sure the infantry picked very many fights either, but once a squad or platoon of them left the base and started poking around, stuff happened. You can be sure that when they called us for 'HELP!' we responded with lethal force.

My primary job at FDC would be to almost instantly locate the target when the calls came in and provide an azimuth for the guns to point within 10 seconds. Then, I would call out the distance to the target and my job was done. After that I could sit back and observe while the other guys managed the rest of the communications and data and mission.

Locating the target was a snap – the guy receiving the call (for help) would call out a six or eight digit coordinate, I'd find it on our large, topographical map, rotate a protractor to that point and read the azimuth off the map. By the 3rd or 4th try I was under 10 seconds. After a couple days, I could do it in 5.

Maybe you're thinking: 'what about the math component? When does that come up?'

Temperature, humidity and wind affect the trajectory of a projectile as well as the explosiveness of the gunpowder – the longer the distance to be traveled, the higher the charge of the propellant, the more critical that effect became. Our 105MM shells would travel up to 7 miles at the maximum charge and once every 3 or 4 hours we'd have to recalculate the possible atmospheric components for future firing data.

In the era before computers that data was computed manually. The math needed to compute those components was really only 4th grade math – the complicated parts of the firing equation had already been meticulously compiled by the Army in a manual. Everyone on the crew would compute a different temperature and humidity level component so we'd have a spectrum of data for the most probable near future conditions.

When a call came in, the 'chief fire director', would check the current temp, humidity and wind and add in the distance to calculate the exact data needed to precisely aim the first rounds. The observer calling us would then adjust our fire as needed.

The guys in FDC seemed to be like-minded in ways other than the incense-burning, guitar-swapping gang though I could have enjoyed the camaraderie of either. Nevertheless, it felt as though my new assignment was a very good fit from the first day.

Time would tell . . .

DAY 134

My shift at the Fire Direction Center consisted of one officer and six *enlisted* guys including me. We were a fairly diverse lot from all around the states. In retrospect, the group seemed to fit the casting mold of a TV sitcom or drama.

Starting with the guy on the far left of the photo . . .

The lieutenant in charge of the *other* shift – I don't remember his name. He happened to still be hanging out in the bunker when I staged this photo. He had a little 'Don Knotts' in him.

He's mock threatening our chief fire director, a Porto Rican guy from the Bronx whose name was (probably) Jamie. Jamie was arguably the smartest and quirkiest guy in the room. He drove a

Cadillac hearse – no, not professionally - as his main set of wheels. He told me it was the perfect *date* vehicle, wink, wink. Jamie was talkative and could be goofy, but when the chips were down in the heat of a fire mission, he was cool-headed, quick-witted and accurately coordinating our fire.

We jumped over Boynton – a sweet guy from down south – Alabama, I think. Boynton was either very polite or didn't have much to say and I never got to know him very well.

The tall blond guy with a bayonet at Jamie's throat is Lieutenant Wilson, the officer in charge of our shift. Wilson was a laid-back Virginian who had spent three months on reconnaissance patrols giving him first-hand experience calling in artillery fire missions. He was an officer, but he was one of us. He didn't pull rank or talk down to us - he didn't act superior and was popular with us regular guys.

Next is Phil, I think. Phil was college material and a good card player, but didn't mind getting his hands dirty. He was a sophisticated Midwesterner – from Pennsylvania maybe?

Then it's Wayne Amaral, a Portuguese fisherman's son from the Boston area. I asked him why he didn't join the Navy and he held up four fingers – their term of enlistment was two years longer than the term for an Army draftee. Wayne had that Boston-area bravado, but was an agreeable guy and hard worker nevertheless. We joked about his 'Ba-stin' accent. I wish I remembered more.

Last, is Theo (I think). From the Midwest (I think) because I don't remember him having any accent. He wasn't our token black – I don't think the Army did that. He was part of FDC because of his intelligence and training. Sorry to say I didn't get to know Theo.

You'll notice barbed wire in the upper right of the first photo – the FDC bunker was the command center and, consequently, had its own protected enclosure within the much larger Fat City firebase.

Lieutenant Wilson in the FDC compound.

DAY 138

Thanksgiving 1968. Vietnam was probably the last place on earth I would have chosen to be that day. Yeah, me and a few hundred thousand other guys . . .

Regardless of the circumstances, a magnificent feast was being served up at our mess tent in Fat City – a Thanksgiving banquet that would have challenged Mom's. Seriously.

I couldn't believe my eyes. It was fabulous! It was so special the Army had even printed menus (see photos) for the occasion.

First to catch my eye were the mixed nuts. Okay, maybe I'm revealing something about myself, but they weren't the 'run-of-the-mill' mixed nuts – it was a deluxe assortment of salted, whole cashews, almonds, Brazil-nuts, hazelnuts and pecans that weren't watered down with peanuts and there were a few gallon tins full of them! And black olives? Who had black olives in 'Nam? And shrimp cocktail - that may have been my first taste of shrimp cocktail. Ever. I was dangerously close to being full before the first bite of T-bird.

The feast was laid out on big, long, cloth-covered tables – everything mom would have served and more. There were large serving tins with piping-hot white and dark roast turkey, real mashed potatoes, stuffing, turkey gravy, glazed sweet potatoes, cranberry sauce, delicious baked rolls and various vegetables. Normally, a line of gruff cooks would plop some of each on your plate like a soup line at a homeless shelter, but not on this occasion - we were allowed to serve ourselves and take as much or as little as we wanted. There was even fresh pumpkin pie with whipped cream for dessert!

As unexpectedly lavish and cordial as it was, I suspected there was more to it - a hidden signification – it was way over the top. Sure, they wanted to boost morale, that was obvious, but it went beyond that. They weren't just saying 'Thanks', they seemed to be saying 'we're sorry'.

The U.S. was conscripting 50,000+ young men each month at that time. Men who mostly did not want to be in the military. Men who's best case scenario would be a two-year interruption of the prime time of their life. Men who were literally putting their life on the line for the sake of a third-world dictator 10,000 miles from home. Any military brass having a conscience couldn't not feel 'sorry' for the suffering they were inflicting.

By November of '68 the 'War' had become unpopular at home. A majority of civilians and more than a few in the military were questioning our objectives as well as our prospects. Nevertheless, the leadership of the U.S. was all in, throwing almost everything it had at Charlie with little indication the tide would ever turn in our favor. Thanksgiving dinner for our troops in Vietnam in '68 would be no different – they were going all out to insure success.

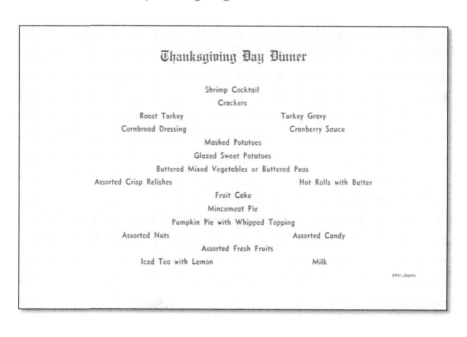

The Thanksgiving Menu for Vietnam in 1968.

DAY 141

The combat fire missions seemed to slow way down after Thanksgiving Day – way, way down - the war kinda stopped. There was talk of a temporary 'cease-fire' through the holidays, but I was skeptical. If Charlie wasn't fighting, it was because he was licking his wounds and/or planning his next move NOT because he was 'ceasing fire'.

The slow down was just fine with us G.I.'s. There wasn't much in the way of *entertainment* in Fat City, but given the choice, we'd all rather just hang out and cross days off the calendar than shoot at Charlie all hours of the night.

DAY 148

Now that the war was on 'hold' so to speak, we in FDC had to find ways to keep busy – stuck working inside of that cramped bunker got boring pretty fast when we weren't shooting.

Naturally, we always had to be at the ready in case Charlie tried to pull a fast one, so there was no letting up regarding our periodic meteorological data computations. Those reports really only took about 15 minutes every 3 or 4 hours leaving us with a LOT of time to kill.

We had an AM radio tuned to the armed forces network which played most of the 'hit singles' from the 'states'. Consequently, I associate: Glen Campbell's 'Wichita Lineman' and Judy Collins' cover of 'Both Sides Now' with those slow times in FDC. They both had a distinctly melancholy quality that captivated as well as haunted me and they seemed to get played at least twice every shift. Today, I cannot hear either song without being immediately transported back to the FDC bunker in November/December of 1968.

Phil offered to teach us to play Bridge. At the beginning, there were 3 of us who signed on, but 2 of those guys (Amaral and Boynton) lost interest leaving me and Phil to play all 4 hands which really doesn't work. It was good fun when we had 4 players, though.

I would sometimes bring my guitar and play/practice. I wasn't comfortable singing, but the guys seemed to appreciate my instrumental renditions of Beatles tunes, Mason Williams' 'Classical Gas' and a self-taught version of Malagueña.

Since our shift worked until 2 AM, we'd get pretty sleepy during the slow times after midnight. Lieutenant Wilson allowed us to sleep as long as we could 'snap to' when a call for help came in. The bunker had a plywood floor and I had enough space by my big map to curl up. It wasn't as bad as it sounds – I'd fold my jacket into a pillow and quickly zonk out.

Captain Alexander was a frequent visitor to FDC. He liked to keep us on our toes and would pop in unannounced to conduct simulated fire missions – on some occasions he'd show up after midnight when we were asleep. He had a stopwatch and timed us. We needed to respond instantly and accurately – I had to have that azimuth for the guns in 10 seconds regardless of the dream I might have been enjoying before he burst in. It sounds reminiscent of Seinfeld's Kramer, but I disciplined myself to immediately switch off sleep and switch on being awake when needed.

DAY 153

Communication in combat is an art form all to itself. On the firebase, phones connected FDC with the CO and each gun via cables and those communications were secure. However, that wasn't the case when talking wirelessly to the battalion HDQ in Chu Lai or with a squad of infantry 5 miles away or to the pilot of a helicopter or a fighter plane. Charlie may not have had our technical expertise or gear, but he had radios, he had translators and he could listen in on our conversations. Consequently, military intelligence conjured up code-names (aka 'call signs') for every individual with communication responsibilities – there must have been hundreds of them in Chu Lai alone.

Also consider: those code names needed to be changed frequently. FDC would receive a new, 'secret' 25-page booklet delivered by hand with the call signs for persons in our area once every couple weeks on average. I remember one occasion receiving a new booklet 48 hours after the last one!

There was a formula for the call sign: it consisted of two totally unrelated words for the guy in charge of an outfit or that plus a number following it for anyone under his command. For example: Captain Alexander might be 'Bloody Newscaster'. Our executive officer might then be 'Bloody Newscaster 2'. Lt. Wilson might be 'Bloody Newscaster 5', etc.

In addition to the secret call signs, intel issued different radio frequencies to be used by different outfits and/or for different functions. We had high and low channels of frequency ranges. Fire missions might be assigned to frequency '34.5 MHz' while requests for medical aid might be assigned to frequency '62.0 MHz'. An infantry patrol leaving Fat City expecting support from Delta Battery, would be instructed which frequency to call us on before they left the base.

Last, but not least there was the phonetic alphabet that all radio communications used. Every letter was represented by a distinctly different sounding 'word' to help eliminate miscommunications. It may sound familiar: 'A' = alpha, 'D' = delta, 'I' = India, 'M' = Mike, 'T' = tango, 'X' = x-ray, etc. I wasn't someone whose job required me to use the radio, but I learned the alphabet anyway seeing as how it became a regular part of military conversation. Somehow, I still remember it.

DAY 156

While life at Fat City was primitive, we nevertheless had all the necessities. There was a gravel road connecting Fat City to Highway 1 and the rest of Chu Lai so our food, drinking water*, ammo, fuel and other supplies were simply trucked in.

* We had both 'potable' and 'non-potable' water at Fat City. We showered in the non-potable stuff until we were on a firebase where it had to be flown in due to the lack of an access road.

Delta Battery (and each outfit stationed at Fat City) made its own electricity. We had two gas-powered generators: a 10 Kilowatt and 5 Kilowatt that ran constantly, 24 hours a day, seven days a week. It was Specialist Blevins' job to make sure they never stopped. Without electricity, we were pretty much dead. Those generators powered all our communications gear, internal lighting and the perimeter floodlights essential to the defense of our portion of the perimeter.

Fat City, like most (if not all) firebases was positioned at the top of a hill. Razor or 'concertina' wire was strung around the entire perimeter of the base to keep Charlie out. *Concertina* wire is a type of barbed wire formed in large coils which are then expanded like a concertina (accordion). Our perimeter lights were positioned inside the wire and pointed outwards to illuminate the wire and anybody who tried to cut their way through it.

I've already described how we showered but another necessity is relieving oneself of the contents of their bladder and bowels. Urination was easiest to deal with: we had a couple eight-inch diameter sections of ceramic pipe strategically embedded in the ground almost perpendicularly that allowed G.I.'s to simply walk up, unzip and pee. Privacy screening? What's that?

Since privacy wasn't a thing and since there were a lot of us, we had a side-by-side, three-seat crapper, aka 'the latrine'. It was a wood-frame construction with a wrap-around screen from the roof down to about chest-level. It wasn't unusual to see all three in use.

The *waste* dropped into cut-off 55-gallon drums with some kerosene in them. The smell of the kerosene more or less neutralized the smell of the crap and after the can filled, it would be pulled out of the outhouse and the kerosene would be ignited to burn up the crap.

Slam, bam that's how it was done in Vietnam! I only pulled that duty on one occasion, but I will never forget it. Ugh.

DAY 159

While we're figuratively twiddling our thumbs waiting for the war to restart, this is as good a time as any to fill the reader in on a few details concerning the 'how' of howitzers. A brief background on the ammunition used will help to better understand and appreciate what's going on.

At this point in December of 1968 our 105MM guns had four types of projectiles: high explosive, illumination, smoke-marker and beehive. Rounds were stored by their respective types in sand-bagged bunkers at each gun emplacement. They were kept shielded from the sun and mostly from the weather.

Combat missions, i.e. those intending to kill the enemy, called for the high explosive (HE) rounds. Each round consisted of four parts - from the top down: the fuse/detonator, the explosive, the shell casing and inside the casing was the gunpowder/charge.

The gunpowder was contained in 7 small cloth sacks (or charges) which were linked to each other with thin cords – the more sacks, the farther the projectile would travel. The fire director in FDC was responsible for calculating how many charges were needed for each mission and relayed that information to the guns – 'charge 1 through charge 7'. The projectile was loosely press-fit into the casing containing the gunpowder. The gunner would separate them, rip off any unwanted charges and reposition the projectile into the casing.

Then the detonator or fuse would be activated – that was the last step prior to shoving the round into the gun's firing chamber.

The illumination round was used for what its name implies: illuminating. The gun would be elevated to its maximum elevation (angle) and fired into the wind. The round carried a magnesium flare connected to a small parachute. The flare would ignite and float down to earth illuminating a football-field sized area for about 60 seconds or less. The only time I saw those used was when we were under attack – more on that later.

The smoke round was used to preset potential nighttime defensive targets during daylight. It produced a big puff of smoke where it landed enabling a spotter to adjust the fire without a lot of noise, risk or expense.

The beehive round was only used when a firebase was under attack from advancing ground troops. Each round contained 6000 fleshettes (think 1" nails with 4 barbs in place of the nail head). The gun would be fired with the barrel pointed level to the ground, directly at the approaching troops. The fleshettes would disperse from the gun nozzle at a 60° angle something like a shotgun blast only FAR more lethal.

While every gun had the high explosive and smoke rounds at the ready, the beehive and illumination rounds were rarely used and were only provided to guns with strategic emplacements. The beehive round could only be used if the emplacement was on the base's perimeter for obvious reasons – guns having an interior placement could not fire beehive rounds, but were perfect for using illumination rounds.

Either of those rounds would only be of use during an attack on the firebase. When that happened, both might need to be fired repeatedly throughout the attack. Thankfully, I only witnessed that once - that story comes later.

DAY 165

Christmas in Vietnam was weird – how could it be anything but? I had never been away from home at that time of year not to mention embroiled in a seemingly pointless war on the other side of the planet in a primitive, third-world, Buddhist country surrounded by virtual strangers. It couldn't have been more foreign. Nothing could have prepared me for the disorientation or my emptiness inside.

Fortunately, my assignment to FDC had emotionally rescued me. For the first time I felt like I had a job to do – a purpose – a value. The job may have been unheroic, but it was safe, I was instantly good at it and the team of guys in FDC made me feel welcome. I didn't realize how lonely I had been until after I had stopped feeling lonely.

One morning, a few days before Christmas, Captain Alexander sent one of our gun commanders (Sergeant Tom) and a squad of us out to search for and procure a Christmas tree - that meant leaving the relatively safe perimeter of Fat City. Tom invited me to tag along and in a moment of boredom and poor judgment, I agreed. After 30 minutes or so of wandering, we discovered an appropriate evergreen and cut it down. Luckily, we didn't stumble across any of Charlie's guys. We were armed, but so what. The five of us could have been ambushed and snuffed in the time it takes to type this.

The few Christmas cards I got cut both ways, reminding me that my family was thinking of me, but also that I was FAR from home in this strange and awful place at this sentimental time of year.

Mom sent a tin of my favorite, chocolate-chip cookies. Aunt Ruby sent an assortment of homemade cookies, too. Both had been reduced to quarter-sized crumbs by the time they reached me, but their thoughtfulness was heartening and the bite-sized crumbs tasted just fine.

Bob Hope was coming to Chu Lai and I was invited to accompany Delta Battery's delegation to see his show on Christmas Eve. That invitation probably wouldn't have been proffered before joining FDC, but my new status and the recent scrutiny I'd undergone must have reassured those in charge of my responsible behavior at such an event.

I was a fan Bob Hope – I loved his deadpan humor, but I was undecided about going. Frankly, I was more interested in witnessing/being a part of history rather than the levity. Or Ann Margret. Or whoever was tagging along on his fifth tour of Vietnam. To my mind it would be like seeing Eisenhower or Churchill or the Beatles in their prime.

On the 'minus' side of the ledger were: the crowd, the risk and the emotional letdown afterwards. I was sure there would be 5000+ G.I.'s at the show - that would put me about a quarter mile from the stage. And that many G.I.'s would HAVE to make it a highly desirable, fairly large target. How hard would it be for VC sappers to lob a few mortar rounds into the middle of us?

Then, after it was over, we'd still be here – the higher Bob uplifted us, the farther we'd fall on the way back to reality.

I decided not to go. Somebody had to stay and mind the store. I was okay with being one of those guys and, in spite of my Christmas tree-hunt recklessness, the first priority was staying alive.

Christmas Day came and it was déjà vu all over again – another 'Thanksgiving Day' feast intended to momentarily distract us from the outrage of our conscripted partnership in this insignificant country's civil struggles.

This time I managed to not fill up on the mixed nuts before the main course.

DAY 168

Part of the feeling of isolation I felt in Vietnam had something to do with the communication technology of 50 years ago. These days we all have a smartphone in our pocket or purse and can instantly ring up a friend across town or in another state or on another continent – no big deal. That was NOT the case in 1968 – FAR from it. Our only means of communication with folks back home was a hand-written letter or a self-recorded cassette. Since it was a war zone, mail would be opened and screened for sensitive info and you'd be lucky if the friend/relative received your post in two weeks.

So when we got the memo informing us G.I.'s of the opportunity to call home via the newfangled Military Affiliate Radio System (MARS), I jumped at the chance.

I had to make a reservation at least two weeks in advance and get transportation from the firebase to the station. I was desperate to call my girlfriend who lived with her parents, so I mailed her the date and time so she could be sure to be home.

I had made the reservation over a month ago and today was the big day. I get a ride to the MARS station in Chu Lai, my turn comes, they ring her up and she answers!

Only one problem: it's not her voice – it sounds as if a robot's synthesized voice is on the other end. The new technology is not perfected – there is a delay of the sound and what I'm hearing doesn't sound human. To make things worse, her mother (who doesn't like me) is there with her monitoring what she says. Real conversation is impossible. We trade a few platonic remarks and say 'goodbye'.

My expectations are crushed.

My elation turns into misery . . .

One of Delta Battery's 105's.

DAY 172

As 1969 rung in and with the holidays behind us, the war was back 'on' again - as if a switch had been thrown - an abrupt awakening after 5 weeks of *ceased fire*.

A couple hours before dusk a call came in urgently requesting artillery support. The guy on the phone had an Aussie accent, but his call sign was in our code book, so Lt. Wilson reckoned he was legit. He sounded desperate and we immediately swung into action with all six guns.

The Aussie was leading a recon patrol that had stumbled onto a much larger force of Viet Cong, were taking heavy fire and were trapped. They needed help NOW. We zeroed in on the coordinates he gave us and a 6-round salvo was on the way in 60 seconds.

He responded: 'Good shooting, mate but those hit behind Charlie. Move them towards us 100 yards!'

Our Fire Director, Jamie adjusted the calculations and relayed the slightly modified data to the guns. Six more rounds were on the way in about 45 seconds.

The Aussie instantly responded: 'Excellent, mates! Move them another 100 yards towards us. Now! Hurry!'

Jamie's face turned pale: 'Are you sure? That puts the rounds close to your position!'

Aussie: 'YES, I'M SURE! FIRE NOW! QUICKLY!'

Jamie looked at Lt. Wilson for permission to comply. Wilson nodded. Our guns are shooting from a distance of about 5 miles – the slightest variation in the wind or mistake by a gunner or calculation by Jamie could be fatal to the recon patrol.

Jamie adjusted the firing data again and relayed it to the guns. Rounds were on the way in 50 seconds.

Lt. Wilson grabbed the mic from Jamie and warned the Aussie: 'Get your heads down!'

FDC held its collective breath - you could hear a pin drop in the bunker. It seemed like it was taking too long for the Aussie to respond.

Suddenly the silence was broken: 'GREAT SHOOTING, MATE! RIGHT ON TARGET! ARMS AND LEGS FLYING EVERYWHERE!'

We were relieved, jubilant and stunned at the same time. Lt. Wilson patted Jamie on the back: "Nice job."

Jamie was indeed relieved and jovially reiterated the Aussie's response for anyone who hadn't heard it.

(continued)

For most (if not all) of us, that was the first time we'd gotten an immediate report of the lethal effect of our collective actions. Under these circumstances, I would have anticipated a victorious cheer, but instead, the mental image created by the Aussie's report had a sobering/mind-numbing effect that muted our reaction.

Corporal Dowdy (back to camera) presides over a fire mission.

DAY 175

One of the oddities of fighting a guerilla war like Vietnam was there were no 'front lines'. Consequently, the next fire mission that came in could be 180° from the last target. With the WWII era howitzers we had initially, the gun crew would have to physically rotate the entire gun – no small feat especially in the rain as the spades at the end of the gun's trails (stabilizing arms) could become embedded in the mud due to the recoil from the shots. When that occurred, the crew would have to dig the spades out before the gun could be rotated.

That's what happened tonight – after the first fire mission completed, a second mission came in requiring some of our guns to be radically repositioned. It had been raining and the crew couldn't dig the trails out fast enough for the guys calling for support, but it couldn't be helped. Ultimately, rounds were in the air in about 7 minutes and, fortunately got there in enough time.

DAY 181

It was late afternoon on a sunny winter day. We (in FDC) were busy setting nighttime defensive targets (Delta Tango's) for an infantry patrol when the Aussie leader of the recon patrol we rescued a few days ago burst into our bunker unannounced. He was a big, genial guy wearing a handlebar moustache and a nonstandard uniform – actually, it didn't look like a uniform. He had dropped in to personally thank every one of us, but especially the fire director, Jamie.

He told us in so many words that he was with us, but not part of us – he was hired by Uncle Sam to do a job. He loved the *adventure* of it all. He was a 'soldier of fortune' – a mercenary.

He told us he thought his number was up when he put that call in to Delta Battery. A company of VC had the five guys of his squad hemmed in. Our immediate, pin-point accuracy saved his patrol. He told us it was some of the finest shooting he'd ever seen. He went around the room and shook everyone's hand and was gone as suddenly as he had come in.

We sat there stunned until the field infantry officer who had been setting the defensive targets prior to the Aussie's interruption broke the silence on the radio with a follow up to his last adjustment. And we were back at work . . .

DAY 187

It sounds unconscionable in today's society, but combat units in Vietnam measured their effectiveness with 'kills', i.e. the bodycount of the enemy they killed. Delta Battery was no different. Captain Alexander had a 'kill board' fixed just outside the door of his bunker. The first time I noticed, it read in the low 100's, but that preceded the introduction of the 'firecracker' round.

Up until then high explosive (HE) was the *go to* ammo for attacking Charlie. The HE round had a 'kill radius' of about 100 feet. Thinking back to the mission with the Aussie mercenary . . . he was calling for HE rounds to be delivered while he and his squad were on the edge of the kill radius.

On that occasion the target was exposed, our guys kept their heads down and we were right on target putting a few more notches on Delta Battery's tally, but that wasn't always the result. More often than not, after the smoke and shrapnel had cleared, our guys surveying the target counted *disappointingly* few kills for us.

All that changed when we started receiving the newly invented 'firecracker' round – another radical innovation I witnessed during my tour of duty.

The firecracker shell carried a large number of golfball-sized bomblets in its projectile. These were ejected at altitude over the target area. Each bomblet then opened 'umbrella-like' fins which spun as they floated to earth. Upon impact, a spring on the bottom threw each bomblet back into the air initiating a short fuse. At about 6 feet above ground, it detonated with the force of a fragmentation grenade. From a distance, the bomblets exploding in quick succession had the sound of a string of firecrackers, hence their name. The results, however were not kid-stuff - within the kill radius, virtually every person was hit multiple times from every side by flying shrapnel - almost no one made it out alive.

Just imagine a volley of six rounds fired at once – the bomblets would blanket an area the size of a football field. There would be no where to hide.

Back then, the description of how it worked sounded like science fiction – today it sounds like an imaginary video game bomb – regardless, the results were real and they were staggering. Our kills went up immediately and within 3 months Delta Battery was at about 450.

DAY 193

Back in the day (before computers) just about anyone who played chess would tell you it was all but impossible to find players you *wanted* to play. Finding someone who knew *how* to play was one thing, finding someone who played at your level was really hard. 'Cause playing someone who beats you every time isn't fun and when the tables are reversed, it's just as bad – not fun.

Nevertheless, if you enjoy the world's most intellectual indoor game, you continue trying to find someone to play. When I put it out to FDC that I played and wondered if anyone else did, I only had one taker: Captain Alexander and I thought to myself: 'uh, oh.' I wasn't expecting my commanding officer to offer to play me – the stakes got quite a bit higher than I had expected.

He obviously had more to lose than I did – if I lost to a West Point grad, our peers would simply think: 'yep, he lost to someone who knew more about strategy.' If the CO lost to a young, lowly specialist, he might also lose some of the respect of his subordinates, i.e. everybody in Delta Battery. Regardless, I couldn't back out now – the game was 'on' and I wasn't going to cave in just because he had more to lose.

Adding to my motivation was the disappointment of not being an officer myself. As a teen, I had fantasized about going to West Point and more recently was denied the opportunity to attend

Officer Candidate School. It was more than just a chess match – it was about my worthiness and qualifications.

At this point I had not yet studied the game of chess – I had played quite a few matches with other guys through the years, but had never read any books on strategy or openings or anything. It didn't seem like Alexander had either.

It was a slow night in our little corner of the war and we played with very few interruptions until he got tired and went to bed. We saved the positions over night and picked up where we left off the next evening.

I was moving (my pieces) very carefully. In spite of the implicit risk, I wanted to win and didn't want to lose because of a stupid mistake. I trusted my opinion regarding his character - that he was not the kind of guy who would abuse his authority over me if I beat him.

Meanwhile, he was good-naturedly complaining about how long it was taking me to move. We hadn't made any kind of arrangement about the speed of the game before we started, so I continued to take as long as I needed.

Gradually, I gained the upper hand and before the second night was over I declared: 'Checkmate'. He was undoubtedly embarrassed and played the 'he-moved-too-slow' excuse while the guys in FDC did their best to not smirk and I gloated in straight-faced silence.

I think that was the end of it, though he refused to play me again.

Yours truly on one of our last days at Fat City.

DAY 196

Speaking of computers, their day had, in fact, just arrived in Delta Battery. Officially known as a 'Field Artillery Digital Automatic Computer', 'Freddy' was intended and destined to make us faster, more accurate and put some of us out of work.

He, or 'it' showed up this day and I was the guy recommended to learn how to use it. I was kind of flattered and said, 'Sure.' We'd all heard of computers, but nobody had actually seen or used one. Little did I realize I didn't really have a choice and my days in FDC were numbered.

I left my big topographical map in the corner and moved into Freddy's driver seat.

Initially, everyone was skeptical about that thing's accuracy and we performed dual calculations for every mission. Once the coordinates of the target were entered, Freddy displayed everything needed to aim the guns in a few seconds: the azimuth, range, charge, elevation, deflection and time of flight.

While I enjoyed my new status of Computer Operator, I felt less valuable and less fulfilled – the skill factor was eliminated - a moron could be taught to operate that thing.

Me, Sergeant Don and his howitzer.

DAY 202

No doubt you've heard the phrase 'hurry up and wait'. It's one I experienced first hand while serving in Uncle Sam's Army, but it didn't always work like that, especially in a combat zone. Today, Delta Battery got orders to move to another firebase and we were moving *today*! Bam! Just like that.

We were moving to LZ Dottie located about 8 miles southeast of Fat City and 5 miles south of Chu Lai – a strategic, small hill with big guns. It was a little further inland and, like Fat City, was accessible by road. Nevertheless, most things in Delta Battery were going to be transported by air via helicopter – the men, the guns, vehicles and everything that was 'air-mobile'.

I was sorry to leave my personalized, private digs at Fat City, but that was life in a 105MM artillery battery in February 1969.

Side note: LZ Dottie was less than a mile from a village named 'My Lai'. LZ Dottie had been the base of operations for the massacre at My Lai on March 16 of '68, the worst atrocity in U.S. military history. This was of no consequence to us because the massacre that had happened eleven months earlier was *unknown* at this time to anyone except those who participated in it. The public (and non-participants) wouldn't find out until November 17th in a New York Times article. Walter Cronkite ran the story three weeks later, December 5th, 1969 on the CBS Evening News.

DAY 203

After arriving at LZ Dottie, I was assigned to bunk with a few guys from a different outfit until other arrangements could be made. That was fine – they kept to themselves and seemed friendly.

Their residence was a bunker built into a hillside. It wasn't as bright and cheery as my old place – it had no windows whatsoever – but it certainly looked like it could withstand the direct hit from rocket or mortar or AK47 fire.

LZ Dottie was just off Highway One and about a mile from MyLai in the lower right corner near the South China Sea.

Once more with feeling!

DAY 206

The FDC crew had been dispersed and was making do with its temporary sleeping quarters at LZ Dottie until today when big timbers for a new bunker arrived. At this point something surprising happened: a couple of them dove into the design and construction of the thing with genuine enthusiasm. I would not have guessed a bridge-player and the son of a fisherman knew how to throw up a bunker, but I was wrong.

Phil and Wayne seemed to know exactly how this sort of thing was done and worked as a team directing the others, like me, who didn't have much of a clue. I was impressed and wondered where they picked up those skills.

A small bulldozer had carved out a space for the bunker - they figured out the foundation, where the timbers went and how to secure them. They/we covered the frame with the materials at hand (plywood, mostly) and then covered that with a gazillion sandbags. It seemed like that many 'cause I was one of the grunts all but endlessly filling them.

The new bunker took maybe three days to build and oddly our executive officer was helping towards the end of the process. At some point on the second day he was standing on the roof and barked an unnecessary order at me that became the first time

(continued on page 116)

While the bunker was going up, I had the idea to take photos of the
various stages from the same perspective (more or less).

116

(continued from page 113)

in my life I remember thinking: 'I'm smarter than that guy – he should be taking orders from me.'

When the construction was done, our new bunker/hootch was a thing of relative beauty. Rock solid and able to preserve its inhabitants from the slings and arrows of Charlie's outrageous fortune. I'm in the doorway of our new bunker.

DAY 215

I started packing for R&R, but my preparations began long ago – as soon as I learned I was being deployed to Vietnam, I looked into this 'R&R' thing. The deal was each G.I. got to take a week off on Uncle Sam's dime at a time of his choosing in one of seven cities: Sidney (Australia), Bangkok (Thailand), Hong Kong, Kuala Lumpur (Malaysia), Singapore, Tokyo (Japan) and Hawaii.*

R&R seemed like an opportunity to experience an exotic, first-world destination and before delving into it, Tokyo, Bangkok, Hong Kong and Singapore were my front runners. Thanks to the Beatles, I had become enamored with Indian Culture – that's 'dots' not 'feathers' – and I discovered Singapore had a large Indian population. In the back of my mind I was thinking about buying a sitar. On top of that, it was a British Crown Colony where they were likely to speak a lot of English. Done.

* These R&R destinations were augmented a bit after 1968. P.S. Hawaii was only available to married G.I.'s rendezvousing with their wives, but I wasn't interested in going there anyway.

When to schedule this little vacay from the war was just about as straight forward – the weather could be something of a factor, but the bigger issue for me: was there a time when Charlie was more likely to attack U.S. bases in Vietnam?

Last year Charlie had mounted a game-changing offensive during Tet – the Chinese New Year. A February edition of LIFE magazine told me everything I needed to know about that. I reckoned he just might try it again and didn't want my bloody corpse displayed in the '69 edition.

Singapore also had lots of Chinese folks, so there would be festivities surrounding the celebration of the New Year that might be fun. I found out Tet in 1969 would start February 17th so it seemed like February 16th would be a great day to for my R&R to begin. Done.

Since I went to the trouble to figure all this out before I even got on the plane to Saigon, I put my request in for February 16th and Singapore as soon as I got the chance after arriving. It wasn't one of the highly requested cities and apparently, the other G.I.'s either didn't think Charlie would try an encore during Tet or simply didn't think about it, so my request was approved without a hitch.

DAY 217

Not only did I plan R&R before getting to Vietnam, I thought about what to wear. I was one of VERY few G.I.'s who brought *civies* to Vietnam. 'Cause who wants to get off the R&R plane in Singapore in military garb?

I'm wearing those civies in Da Nang (from where the flight to Singapore departed) and I didn't anticipate the razzing I'd take from a Marine. Once I was in the terminal, I got up to the counter and a PFC issuing boarding passes says, 'Oh, A DOG FACE!' as he inspects my papers. Maybe he thought I was a civilian contractor because of the clothes? I'm completely blind-sided - aren't we on the same side? Anyway, he's in his element surrounded by other JAR HEADS and I'm out of mine, so I say nothing and get on the airliner.

It's a thousand miles to Singapore and ALL of us are eager to get this party started so we couldn't get there soon enough.

After landing, we were whisked to the hotel arranged and paid for by the Pentagon. Thank you very much, Sirs.

A new buddy from the flight, suggested we get massages. I'm thinking, 'Exotic experience'? Yes, indeed.

So, we find the 'massage room', get naked and climb on separate massage beds. I'm lying on my stomach under a towel with this rather large, unattractive woman rubbing me almost everywhere. Then, I'm on my back as she's working on parts neighboring other parts which elicit the 21-year old's, haven't-been-with-a-woman-in-eight-months, involuntary, male response. I was hoping she didn't notice, but she does and asks, "Oh, you want 'happy ending'?"

My face was beginning to glow bright red, as I blurted out, "No, thanks", while gathering the towel around me and making my getaway.

Of course, I *did* want a 'happy ending' I just didn't want *that* one. The urge to have sex with someone, *almost* anyone was over-powering.

Sex - it's what G.I.'s did on R&R – an implicit rite. The term 'R&R' wasn't just a misnomer, it was a euphemism. Nobody *rested* on R&R. You're in a foreign country – everybody's a stranger you'll never see again – it's the perfect scenario for unaccountability. Every guy returned from his weeklong vacay with tales of the girl(s) he slept with. Some even had photos.

Don't get me wrong, my motivation had *nothing* to do with peer pressure – my hormones were raging as much as any 21-year olds' and my participation in that activity was long overdue. Though I was not a virgin, my singular experience had been less than satisfying. I had some catching up to do.

Outside our hotel, my new buddy and I hailed a cab. Once inside, we inquired about where we might locate eligible women. He knew exactly where to take us.

The evening went as I had hoped and by the next morning I no longer felt like I was playing catch-up to my fellow G.I.'s in this department of life. Sorry, no photos.

The lion seemed to be the symbol of Singapore.
This one graced the foyer of my hotel.

DAY 218

After I bid little Miss Singapore fond adieu and enjoyed breakfast
(like never before), I was off to my next R&R objective: SHOPPING.
G.I.'s on R&R bought stuff - LOTS of stuff – custom tailored suits
and hifi gear were our most common *souvenirs*, but I wasn't most
G.I.'s – I came to Singapore for a sitar.

I don't remember having a plan of attack for finding the sitar, but it
didn't matter 'cause I met a local guy in the lobby of the hotel who
offered to show me around. His name was Jess Singh - he was
about my age, spoke perfect English and was neatly dressed. I
thought: 'giddy-up!'

I told Jess I wanted to buy a sitar and he replied, 'Okay, but what
about a custom suit?' That should have been a clue regarding his
motives, but it flew right by me. 'Yeah, I could use a sport coat.'
Naturally, he knew just the place to get it and we hopped in a cab.

The shop he took me to was nicer than any I'd ever visited in the
states and he disappeared while a couple older guys took my
measurements. They brought out quite a few different materials
and I picked a tan cashmere for a traditional sport coat. Then they
showed me some crazy new patterns – a shiny blue paisley caught
my eye. I had them make a second coat using that, but in the new
'Nehru' style with the short, upright collar and more buttons up

the front. They told me to come back tomorrow to pick them up and it was time for lunch.

Jess reappeared and asked me if I'd ever had Malaysian food. I said, "No," and he told me I HAD to try it. I thought: 'when in Malaysia, eat like a Malaysian!'

We cabbed it to a building that didn't look like a restaurant, but after climbing some stairs there it was, a rather simple, large white room with a big open balcony facing a small, tropical forest at the far end. They showed me to a table near the balcony, facing the forest, Jess ordered my food and disappeared again.

I had no idea what to expect. For starters they placed a large banana leaf in front of me where the plate normally goes and left a small dish with a few layers of bread-like food. Then a large multi-sectioned tray showed up with different curries in each little section. The waiter made a gesture like I should use the bread to scoop up the curries, bowed with his hands folded in front of him, and said, "Namaste" as he left.

I still wasn't sure that's what he meant, but I looked around and saw a guy using the bread as an eating utensil and thought: 'Cool, that must be what I'm supposed to do.'

Until that point in my life, food wasn't such a big deal. I was *gaga* for my mom's slow-cooked pork roast with mashed potatoes, pork gravy and boiled carrots, but eating was pretty much just something you did three times each day to give your body energy.

Then I took a bite of this little pile of green stuff on the bread and my opinion of food changed forever. I tried a second curry which produced another 'Wow'. A third had a very different flavor, but was yet another new taste sensation. There were six or seven different curries – some I loved and some I liked, but the experience was fantastic. I mopped up every morsel with the bread.

I started to look around the room when Jess magically appeared and wondered "where to next." I told him I was interested in visiting Hindu and Buddhist temples.

He thought that was a curious request, but said, "We're walking distance from a couple."

Jess escorted me to two Hindu temples.

They were both dark, windowless places with statues of Hindu gods, burning incense, some food on a plate on the floor and horizontally symmetrical altars at one end.

(continued)

The first temple had florescent lighting and white tiled walls giving it an incongruous subway station feel. Its tall, lean, youthful Brahmin looked like a hippie from San Francisco in a brief loincloth with unkempt hair down to his waist.

The other, darker temple resembled a scene out of an 'Indiana Jones' movie. It was presided over by a bald Brahmin in his fifties who seemed to be preoccupied with the performance of some ritual. He wore a white, floor-length skirt and acted like we weren't there. I felt an unfriendly, unwelcome *presence* in his temple and was relieved to go back on the street.

The differences of these two temples located on the same block made me think that Christianity wasn't the only religion with different interpretations and expressions.

After we left the second temple Jess told me that was all he had time for, but tomorrow we'd shop for the sitar.

He arranged with our cabbie for us to take the scenic route back to my hotel - through the old Chinese section decorated for the New Year festival and crossing a river teeming with sampans like a scene out of a National Geographic documentary.

Sampans on the water in Singapore.

DAY 219

After breakfast I walked outside my hotel to meet up with Jess and noticed a couple turbaned guys sitting cross-legged on the sidewalk across the street – snake-charmers. I could see the snakes from my vantage point – one a very large cobra with its hood flared, swaying to the movement of the snake charmer's flute as it lay on the pavement! Ethnic busking like that was part of the reason I choose Singapore, but as keenly as I wanted a closer look, the possibility of a snake losing interest in the flute and slithering towards me was a concern. I got no closer. (continued)

Jess arrived about then and we hailed a cab. I asked him about the dangers of these snakes, but he wasn't concerned and told me it really wasn't a problem. That didn't change my mind about taking a closer look one single bit - Jess took the photo.

The musty music shop he took us to didn't seem like much from the street, but inside was a different story. It had a number of sitars hanging on the wall with a variety of other Indian musical instruments crammed into every available inch. Besides sitars, there were veenas, tamburas, bansuris, and tablas and more that I couldn't name - the virtual 'Sitar Center' of Singapore.

Almost too many sitars to choose among.

I was uninformed about the quality of the instruments and had to put my trust in their recommendation. I picked a gorgeous sitar with a gourd at both ends. We arranged for it to be shipped to my parents' house in Illinois. The total cost was about $350 including crating.

This shop had all kinds of other hand-crafted items from India and I couldn't resist also buying a chess set and a two-foot tall hookah, though I never used either one for their intended purpose. The chess set was attractive, but non-standard and unacceptable in tournament play. I would have used the hookah, but the bowl was huge – too large to smoke anything of value and I made it into a lamp.

After today's shopping spree we needed to revisit the haberdashery to retrieve the blazers I bought yesterday. I had more *souvenirs* than planned and they would be returning to Vietnam with me.

While driving, Jess invited me to his parents' house for dinner to get a real, home-cooked Indian meal. By then we had earned each other's confidence and, honestly, I was as eager to eat there as I was flattered by the invitation.

His family lived in a very large, very plain apartment complex that resembled the tenement housing developments of Chicago. Their tiny apartment was furnished much like any in the United States except for a diminutive Hindu shrine in one corner. Jess' mom didn't really speak English, but was friendly and seemed to be honored by my visit. Jess had a couple younger siblings that paid little or no attention to me.

Honestly, the meal didn't live up to my expectations – there was a dumpling thing and something like a stew which didn't taste at all like the curries I had at the restaurant. It was the gesture that mattered most and was as memorable as any restaurant I visited.

Before the night was over, Jess and I exchanged addresses, shook hands and promised to stay in touch.

Singapore street scene.

DAY 220

I'm on my own for day number three of R&R. I perused the hotel's little collection of travel brochures for suggestions of things to see. The Botanic Gardens looked interesting.

It was mid-morning when I arrived and the big park was all but empty. I'm thinking 'great' I've got the place to myself. As I'm going through the turn-style somebody suggested I might want to feed the chimpanzees. They were selling bags of peanuts in the shell for a buck and I thought, 'sounds like fun'.

It turns out the chimps were not in cages or behind fences – they were allowed to run free throughout the park. Well, that's 'different', I thought.

Sure enough, I get about 200 feet into the park and there's a small band of about six chimps trotting towards me. Great!

As they approached I thought I'd feed them from my hand. I hadn't received any instruction or caution regarding their 'feeding' so I thought 'why not'? I held out a single peanut in the palm of my right hand while clutching the bag near my chest with the left as the group's leader got closer.

He got within about 6 feet and suddenly, with zero hesitation, like a lightning strike, he lunged at me, deftly snatched the bag of peanuts from my left hand and raced away with the other chimps chattering their gleeful approval.

For the split second he was lunging at me I couldn't believe what was happening – I was totally taken off guard. By the time I reacted it was over. I chased after them and naturally, that was useless. Luckily, it seemed as though no one had witnessed me getting outsmarted by an inferior species.

I guess I should be thankful the only thing they injured was my pride.

The garden's orchids were my consolation. This Chicagoan had never seen an orchid much less acres of them. There was an almost endless variety of petals and colors - the world's largest collection growing in the wild. Mind-blowing.

DAY 221

The thing to do this day seemed to be 'Tiger Balm Garden', an outdoor theme park filled with historical Chinese dioramas and moralistic Buddhist propaganda. As I approached the entrance a young Chinese guy approached and offered to be my guide. This time I declined.

The 'garden' was a bit of a weird place. It had a number of static scenes depicting gory battles and visions of Buddhist hell. I wish I had that day back – I'm sure I could have found something better to do.

DAY 223

The first thing I wondered when I got back to Vietnam was, "did Charlie attack LZ Dottie while I was gone?" "Yes," was the response and I felt darn good about my choice of dates for R&R. No one had been injured in the rocket attack on the first day of Tet and there wasn't any real damage.

Before I could pursue the subject further, I was informed by Lieutenant Wilson that I was being *rewarded* for my *good behavior* and would resume my duties as the Delta Battery 'supply guy' in Cherry Hill. He said that "they had been watching me," that I had earned the position back and I think he shook my hand. He told me to pack my stuff and take the next chopper headed back there.

This news came as a complete surprise. Trading the firebase for the cushy life at safe and secure Cherry Hill seemed like an upgrade until I remembered how lonely I had been there and how unsatisfying my duties would be.

Nevertheless, it was an *order* not an *offer* and I knew it was safer there so I didn't object. I bid my FDC buddies farewell, stuffed everything into my duffle bag and flew to Cherry Hill that same day.

My old cot was still there waiting for me, but occupying the other side of the hootch was 'Mary' not Homer.

'Mary' was his nickname, of course – I don't remember his real name - it might have been 'Tim'.

I've *flashed forward* by sharing this bit of gossip. Tim had been given the nickname, as you might guess because of his sexual preference and his flamboyant personality.

Welcome back to Cherry Hill, Specialist Baskin. Here's another curve ball for you to swing at. (Would *screwball* make a better metaphor? Maybe that depends on your knowledge of baseball.)

Tim on his cot.

DAY 229

By the end of my first week back at Delta Battery's outpost on Cherry Hill, someone had *clued me in* about my new roommate. I know in this day and age it sounds impossibly naïve, but he was the first openly gay man I'd ever met and, honestly, for a while I doubted the rumor was true. It was hard for me to believe and harder yet to understand. Remember: this is 1969.

He and I were lying on our bunks reading before nodding off and Tim *opened up* to me – opened up and then some. He asked me if I had heard about his nickname. I responded in the affirmative and, long story short, before the conversation had ended he confirmed the rumors and offered me his services 'if I ever had the urge to try something different'.

I wasn't exactly sure what that meant, but I visualized things I couldn't imagine myself doing and took a pass. That was the last time we talked about it.

DAY 232

My sole responsibility at Cherry Hill was Delta Battery's laundry – at least that's what I remember. The dirty clothes came in via chopper, I'd transport them to our laundry facility and reverse the process when they were done. That was maybe twice a week and once again I'm wondering to do with all my free time.

I have no idea what Tim was supposed to be doing, but it wasn't my job to keep tabs on him and I didn't really care. He disappeared every day just like Homer had.

He told me he spent his evenings at the NCO club which seemed unlikely but I never went there to see for myself – talking with strangers while sipping over-priced beer was not my thing.

Meanwhile, I was either flying below the KP duty radar or my number just didn't come up before getting reassigned to a firebase, but you're gonna have to hold that thought for a few days . . .

DAY 237

Boring is where *lazy* intersects the *unimaginative. Unboring* isn't complicated, it just requires a little 'out-of-the-box' thinking. The sign above the entrance to our hootch was boring, 'mil-spec' dreck and I decided to do something about it. By then I had forgotten the 'awning incident'.

Before enlisting I had studied a little calligraphy – Mrs. Zahler set that ball in motion in 7th grade at Central Middle School. Naturally, we had learned how to print in first grade, but Zahler taught us the proper proportions of each letter and helped us/me to appreciate the importance of a uniform style.

My dad valued fine penmanship and loved the elaborate, Old English typeface. He had introduced it to me long ago and produced a signpost with our family name in Old English. Then, a couple months before getting on the bus to basic training at Ft. Leonard Wood, I met a guy who taught me how calligraphy was done with pen and ink. I bought a book of typefaces and a set of pens and had learned how to use them.

I took down the signboard above our hootches' door with glee, covered it with a bright, red enamel and painted my old English 'D' in contrasting white 'free hand'. Then, I added the decorative, psychedelic filigree, 'elta' to its center and the word 'supply' underneath.

When I renailed it above the door, it was a thing of beauty.

Take that conformity! Boring no more!

My buddy, Sergeant Don was passing by on
his way to R&R just after I put it up.

DAY 244

A home-made recording of a new rock band arrived today from my girlfriend (and future wife) – the group called themselves 'Led Zeppelin' which seemed like an obvious attempt to ride 'Iron Butterfly's' coattails. She had made the tape using a portable (cassette) recorder by holding a cheap microphone up to the loudspeakers as the LP played on her friend's turntable.

I was happy to receive anything from her – it didn't happen often enough. She was fairly excited about these guys and their music in the letter that accompanied the tape. It named Jimmy Page as the guitarist and leader.

I was skeptical about a band I'd never heard of even if Page (who I'd seen LIVE with the Yardbirds) was in it. I had a little portable cassette player, too and I listened to the tape immediately.

In spite of just about the lowest fidelity possible I was captivated by what I heard. They had me with the first two notes. This was radically new music. A blend of raw blues, distorted power chords and psychedelics unlike anything I'd heard before – darker and more powerful than Cream. I listened to the recording all the way through, reread the letter and listened to it again. It was stunning – a game-changer.

On one hand I was thrilled, but on the other I was upset. Music was on the move back in the real world – this could be the tip of the iceberg - and I was missing it. This album alone would take *rock* in a new direction and I wouldn't be there to witness the new trend.

Why now? Why me? I was pointlessly pinballing from one nonessential job to another – from one thumb-twiddling duty assignment to the next - stuck in this meaningless conflict for the next four months and helpless to do anything about it.

The Captain's driver, Danny (?)

DAY 251

It was a beautiful Sunday at Cherry Hill and I had arranged to borrow a vehicle from the motor pool to go to the beach in Chu Lai. I didn't want to be alone, but I don't think I invited anyone to go with so I was solo. I didn't want to drive a 2½-ton truck either, but that's what was available and I took it.

I had been to the beach before and remembered the route to a stretch I liked. No one but me showed up that particular, glorious Sunday – I had the whole beach to myself.

I drove that big ugly truck down the beach at least a half-mile and parked. The Marine air base was somewhere on the other side of the sandy ridge that ran parallel to the shore about 300 feet inland. Guard bunkers were spaced every 500 feet or so along the top of the ridge and I felt the eyes of Jar Heads on me.

I don't really swim and the waves with possible rip tides kept me close to the shore. It was interesting to have the beach to myself, but it really wasn't much fun to be alone and a bit eerie. Within an hour I was ready to go back.

The truck started fine, but I had backed into some loose sand and it wouldn't move. Having grown up in Chicago, I had experience with *rocking* the vehicle back and forth to escape from deep snow, but that technique wasn't working. After about 20 minutes of spinning the wheels, I realized: I was stuck.

146

Now what?

I could walk up to one of those guard bunkers to get help, but they would be staffed with Marines and I had just gotten a taste of their attitude toward Army guys. Who knows, they might shoot me.

So I walked back the way I came. There had been an MP in a guard house at the entrance and the guy on duty called my motor pool who told him they'd send somebody right out.

I got back to vehicle about the time they pulled up in a second deuce and half (truck). They were none to happy to see me - I must have broken up their card game.

Their truck had a motorized winch which they hooked up to the front bumper of my truck. I got behind the wheel and between their winch and my rear wheels, I got out easily. I drove it back and told them I was sorry, but they were not appeased.

I thought, 'oh well, what real harm was done?' and took it easy for the rest of the day.

More famous last words . . .

DAY 253

My buddy Keith showed up at the back door of our hootch with a full duffle bag in tow late in the morning. I was happy to see him but disappointed with his news: he was replacing me at Cherry Hill. Apparently, my assignment had come with a narrow margin of error and the stuck truck screw-up put me back on the CO's shit list. So, it was back to the field for me.

Keith performing his normal military job.

DAY 254

So begins the third and final act of my Vietnam duty.

During my recent stay at Cherry Hill, Delta Battery had moved again and was now dug in atop LZ Buff about two miles further inland from LZ Dottie. There were zero roads or even water buffalo trails to or from Buff so everything had to be transported by helicopter.

I got placed into a small, bunker/barracks with about five other guys. My new home was conveniently located near the command bunker of Captain Alexander and the center of the firebase. I had the bottom bunk, the CO's driver, (whose name might have been) Danny had the top.

Delta Battery shared the crescent-shaped hill with 'A' Company of 1/52nd Infantry and 'B' Company, 26th Engineers – a gully separated us from them. They were situated on the north and east sides of the crescent, while Delta Battery had its six guns spread out side-by-side running along our southern perimeter.

A gravel/dirt road ran down from our side of the hill south to a flat space outside the perimeter of razor wire that would become my new office, the Landing Zone.

DAY 255

My first choice of jobs at LZ Buff would have been to rejoin FDC, but there would be no choice of jobs this time. I was assigned to help another guy (Harold?) haul the daily shipments of ammo and supplies up from the landing zone and distribute it to the battery.

When I was told about my new assignment, I thought: Ugh. Low brow, grunt work. Apparently, they were genuinely unhappy with me - Captain Alexander had a very different point of view and obviously didn't appreciate mine. This may have been his career but by now he should have known it was NOT going to be mine. Like most G.I.'s I was simply counting the days until I went home and THEN I would be counting the days until I was freed altogether. If he couldn't see any humor in my getting the truck stuck on the beach, he should put himself in therapy to see if he *had* a sense of humor.

Yes, of course, Vietnam was a *life and death* assignment but sheesh, give me some slack – do we have to sweat the infinitesimally small stuff?

Anyway, I got the message and I was likewise genuinely unhappy with my job assignment. I had about 100 days remaining and it was going to be hard work from here on out.

DAY 256

My new work partner, Harold was a decent guy. Lean like me, fairly smart and willing to work hard. He even played chess. He had a bit of a drawl and was from somewhere near the Mason-Dixon line - Kentucky, I think.

We drove the battery's ¾ ton truck down to the landing zone together while he explained our duties. "Choppers drop off their load, we haul it up the hill and deliver it where it's supposed to go. When something is being shipped back to Chu Lai (or wherever), we get that down to the LZ and one of us hooks it up to (the underside of) the chopper while it hovers."

It sounded simple enough and turned out to be fairly straightforward. That last bit about 'hooking containers to choppers while they hovered' stirred something in me. The thought of doing that gave me a rush of adrenaline for reasons I could not and cannot imagine. In a word it was 'dangerous' and there haven't been many things in my life that I knew had the potential for disaster that I chose to pursue.

Most of the supplies each day consisted of ammo for the six howitzers. The rounds came two per crate weighing about 120 pounds per container. I wanted to neatly stack them on the truck bed, but Harold didn't. I thought, okay, whatever works, but sometimes we had to make multiple trips because we didn't stack them neatly in the first place. The careless throwing of the ammo was either Harold's way of expressing his disdain for this place and this assignment or he didn't appreciate *order* as much as me.

Each gun had a slightly different allotment – some got illumination rounds, some got beehive rounds, some needed more high explosives, some needed less, etc. We'd drive up, ask that gun's commander what was needed and throw it off the truck forming an untidy pile near his gun. His guys (the guys assigned to that gun) were responsible for putting the various rounds where they belonged. The five different projectiles were all kept separate to avoid confusion during tense fire missions and the guys on each gun knew best where they belonged.

After the ammo was passed out, we were done for the day as long as there wasn't a water tanker or other supplies that needed to be hauled up and delivered.

DAY 257

After day's work was done, dinner eaten and the sun had set, I went looking for those guitar-playing buddies I abandoned in favor of FDC a few months earlier. I poked around the gun emplacements and, Voila! Found 'em in one of the bunkers.

There were a couple new faces mixed in with the guys I already knew. Nobody asked where I'd been 'cause in this little outfit everybody knew everything about everybody that they cared to know. If they didn't know, it was because they didn't care.

The radio was on, a *dubbie* was going around and a new guy who looked like he coulda been a rock star was playing a Gibson six-string acoustic - the first real guitar I had seen here. My ears perked up at the sound of his playing. When he sang, I thought: he's either a rock star or will be. He was good-looking, had a smooth tenor voice, the confidence of a performer and knew his way around a six-string.

His name was (probably) Robert, he was the gunner on the Quad 50 attached to the 1/52 Infantry for the defense of LZ Buff.

The guitar made its way to me. I wanted to make an impression, so I played my version of 'Classical Gas'. I think I followed that with 'Masters of War'. I couldn't sing at the level of Robert but I could whine like Dylan. Then it was somebody else's turn and I passed the Gibson to the left. (continued)

153

(continued from 151)

I don't remember the conversation that followed, but it was cool and friendly. I mostly listened. At some point Robert needed to get back and I left shortly after that.

Robert in the gunner's seat making sure the
Quad 50 is ready to go.

DAY 258

By now I've been on the new job for a few days, observing Harold's technique hooking up the outgoing shipments and I'm itching to try it myself. I tell him to let me do the next one and he's fine with that. "There's only one thing you gotta remember," he says, "DON'T grab the hook on the underside of the chopper! It's gonna have a big static charge and will knock you on your ass! Hold the noose *still* with both hands and wait for the chopper to line up, then loop it over the hook."

'I got this', I thought.

We spent quite a bit of our time each day waiting on the LZ for the choppers to arrive. You'd hear them in the distance before you could see them. There were four primary types of choppers we dealt with: the Huey, the Chinook, the Bell and the Flying Crane. By now probably every one of us could identify which it was by its own unique sound.

Most of the gear we shipped was via the dual-rotor Chinook. It was the size of a flying school bus with a rotor at each end on top.

When they came in the wash of the blades sent sand flying everywhere - small rocks became projectiles. We'd take cover until it was close to being overhead and then race over to the load.

I jumped on top of the tanker being sent back and held the noose high just like Harold said. With the chopper directly overhead, I'm in the eye of the propeller wash – the wind is more or less calm, but the noise of the chopper's two motors is deafening.

That's me 'hooking up' a water tanker.

The pilot of the Chinook is located at the front of its fuselage facing the opposite direction; he has zero visibility of me. One of the chopper's crew lies on the floor inside looking down through an opening just behind the hook and directs the pilot.

At this moment a gust of wind or motor malfunction or RPG attack from Charlie would cause the chopper to suddenly veer and possibly crush the guy holding the noose – in this case, me.

I snagged the hook and jumped off the tanker. The Chinook eased upward until the straps were tight and off it went.

Man, that was exciting! What a rush!

I WANNA DO THAT AGAIN!

And I did. Oblivious to the danger, about 50 times in all, throwing caution to the wind after all that talk about playing it safe.

A 105 setting defensive targets in the afternoon on LZ Buff.

DAY 260

. . . was a sunny, hot, April day. We received so much ammo it took two truck loads to get it all delivered. After we had finished, the water trailer still needed to be brought up and Harold had something else to do. No problem, I got this.

I drove down to the LZ, hooked the trailer to the truck and drove up the hill. I parked more or less where I'd seen Harold park and unhooked it. What I didn't notice was Harold *always* set the brakes on the trailer before unhooking it from the truck. I was parked on a slight incline and the trailer immediately started to roll backwards.

There is no stopping a fully-loaded, 400-gallon tanker rolling down hill and I/we were very fortunate no one was in its path, but that's as much luck as I had that day.

It quickly picked up speed following the downward curvature of the gully and flipped over at the bottom. In spite of being sealed, the water gushed out its top.

It wasn't a total loss, but what water remained would need to be used for drinking and cooking – no showers that night.

Once again my journalistic instincts inspired me to photograph the incident which seems odd 50+ years later. Naturally, I was embarrassed over the mistake and yet, as you can see I didn't feel the need to participate in righting the trailer. I guess I figured there were enough other guys already taking care of that and besides, I seriously wanted to disappear.

I didn't make that mistake again.

DAY 262

It may sound weird to say this, but I think LOTS of guys like to witness and/or trigger explosions and I'm one of them. I can't help but wonder if there was something in my responses to the Army's entrance exam that tipped them off about that particular proclivity of mine and influenced my assignment to the artillery. I'll never know . . .

In my time *off duty*, I'd hang around the guns (like I did at Fat City) hoping to get the chance to pull the lanyard. Of course, that was at least partly due to the exceedingly few other activities on our little island of howitzers, but I thought it was a *hoot* to watch them in action and a thrill to fire them.

As time went on, I became an irregular part of Sergeant Don's crew, showing up most afternoons to see if I could *help*. Don even taught me how to aim the gun – i.e. do his job.

I never loaded the gun, though – that looked hazardous. After shoving the round into the chamber, a different guy closed the breach behind it – the breach mechanism was like a guillotine and I was too fond of my fingers to risk a beginner's mistake.

But pulling the lanyard was a BLAST! (Sorry, I couldn't resist)

One day as I watched a fire mission from the sidelines, the guy closing the breach (Glen) thought he hadn't closed it properly and re-grabbed the lever at the exact moment the gunner pulled the lanyard. They were firing with charge 7 (having the biggest recoil), Glen was violently flung back, his shoulder was instantly separated and his forearm broken. At the time I was thinking he was lucky that was the extent of it.

Glen was medivac-ed that afternoon to the hospital in Chu Lai and his tour of duty may have been over - we never saw him again.

Me playing gunner in the afternoon.

DAY 275

There were rewards and consequences for being a leading-edge baby boomer. Most of us were our parents' first child and had to deal with their elevated expectations and experimental child-rearing techniques. We were in the first wave of kids whose parents fled the city for a new life in a new tract house in the suburbs. We were the first of the generation raised watching TV. We were the first of the generation whose parents were influenced by Benjamin Spock's 'The Common Sense Book of Baby and Child Care'.

More personally, I was a member the first class to attend our town's brand new high school all four years. Then, I enrolled at the Chicago Circle campus of the University of Illinois in the first quarter after it was inaugurated. Regrettably, I was in the first wave eligible for the new military draft in August of 1964, exactly 18 years after the beginning of the baby boom.

Since joining the U.S. Army in January of 1968, I personally experienced a few more *firsts*. Some were game-changers: the M16, a war fought with helicopters, the first use of solid-state computers in the artillery and on this day we received six brand new 105MM howitzers to replace our WWII/Korean Era guns.

I imagine one might feel the new M102 is least of the *firsts* mentioned and I wouldn't disagree, but on this day in Vietnam in 1969 it was significant. The new, modernized 105MM howitzer was much better suited to our conflict, a war without fronts. It was 1/3rd lighter than the old gun meaning a smaller chopper could transport it further and it swiveled 360 degrees on a newly incorporated base which made the gunner's task easier when the next mission came in with an azimuth 120° (or more) away from the last. It was another first in a string of them for me.

DAY 281

There was a rumor going around that the Republic of South Vietnam had an army – an army that was actively defending their country, but up until now I had not seen ANY evidence of such a thing. Lo and behold, on this day a few of them showed up on LZ Buff with a 105MM howitzer. They had uniforms and rifles, too!

It seemed like they were visiting to learn something from us *pros*. One of our guns simulated a fire mission from 'contact' to 'rounds in the air' in our usual, under-one-minute efficiency. Then it was their turn.

We watched as they fumbled with this or that. There was some shouting and some hand waving while several of them simply stood around. Eventually, a round was loaded. There was more twiddling of knobs and some discussion and about ten minutes after the coordinates had been received, they finally got the round off. The Keystone Cops could have done almost as well.

At that point I felt like I understood one of the reasons we were here, but so what? Their incompetence didn't justify U.S. commitment, expense and sacrifice.

That night I/we had a second encounter with them. Well into the night after everyone in my bunker was asleep, one of them crept in.

Danny was partially awake in the bunk above me and the intruder made a slight noise as he snuck up to our bed. Danny saw him reach for my new, portable radio sitting near my head and yelled, "Hey! What are you doing?!"

The guy was reaching across my face in the dark as I opened my eyes. At Danny's alert, he instantly turned and made his getaway, while I struggled to understand what was happening.

For a second I thought he was intending to kill me.

My heart was pounding as Danny told us, "He was going to steal your radio."

All's well that ends well. I thanked Danny and we did all roll over and go back to sleep though it took me a little longer than the others. I couldn't help but wonder if those guys and that one in particular were representative of their army.

A couple days later, their contingent left LZ Buff and we never saw them again.

DAY 284

It was a gorgeous day – clear skies, a slight breeze and temps in the low 80's. The war had gotten slow and Captain Alexander wanted to keep us on our toes. Delta Battery had these new guns and he wanted to see how well the six gun-crews knew how to use them.

He gathered everybody together after lunch to announce a contest. He pointed toward a small house near the southern horizon and told us, "This is a 'turkey shoot' – that's the target. The first gun to hit it wins a case of beer and barbequed steaks for their crew."

The small assembly cheered its approval!

"No coordinates," he continued, "No help from FDC. Use 'bore-sighting'. Fire smoke rounds. Any questions? Okay. Get to your guns, point them at the house and wait for my signal."

I was thrilled. This was gonna to be FUN!

I had a front row seat for this once in a lifetime event – I sat facing the little house/target on the short stack of sandbags that ringed Sergeant Don's gun. From my vantage point, five of the guns were in my peripheral vision.

When every gun was ready, the CO yelled, "Fire at will!"

The six howitzers fired all but simultaneously. A couple were fairly close to the target. They each made adjustments and fired again in about 15 seconds. These rounds were closer but there were still no 'hits'. It was fantastic!

More adjustments made and another set of rounds fired. By the third volley, the guns weren't firing in unison and it was easy to see which gun produced which blast of smoke by the target.

Bulls-eye! The fourth round resulted in a direct hit by one of the guns. Sergeant Tom's crew cheered their victory and I was disappointed it had ended so quickly.

The BBQ'ed steak smelled impossibly good later that evening as I walked by returning from the mess tent, but I wasn't jealous – I was happy for Tom and his crew. I was still over the moon as a result of witnessing that awesome display of firepower.

Bill (or Jim?), Corporal Dowdy and his howitzer.

DAY 288

We had a big load of ammo and supplies coming in today so Harold and I made it down to the LZ early. I brought my portable radio for entertainment while we waited (for the choppers to arrive) and tuned in as the Armed Forces DJ launched his morning show: 'Gooooood Morning, Vi-et-nam!' I had heard his idiotic monologue before and hated it. It might be a 'good morning' in the secure, comfortable confines of a Saigon military radio station, but out here in the 'you-could-be-killed-any-minute-real-war', it stunk of a feeble, transparent attempt to boost morale and I couldn't buy it.

The DJ who originated that slogan, Adrian Cronauer, was long gone by the time I got to Vietnam, but his legacy was being perpetuated by G.I.'s following in his footsteps. Twenty years later, when Hollywood made the movie with Robin Williams playing the part of Cronauer, the edge was off and I was able to enjoy it somewhat, but there was nothing *good* about any morning in Vietnam in 1969.

That morning I remember hearing Deep Purple's 'Hush' for the first time. The tinny, portable radio's speakers forced me to imagine the fat, growling tone of their guitars and reminded me once again how much I missed the world outside of this pathetic country. 77 days to go. Ugh.

DAY 290

Another day spent humping ammo and another evening spent with my guitar-buddies. Robert was there with his Gibson while I had brought my cheap Vietnamese knock off. After playing his Gibson with its rich tone, I mentioned how great it was to play a real guitar and out of the blue, he offered to trade me. He was willing to take my crap guitar plus my nearly new portable radio in a swap.

My first thought was 'he's got to be joking with me', but no, he was ready to make the trade. My second thought was, 'I can buy another radio just like this one at the PX,' and before he changed his mind, I agreed to the deal.

Nobody had a real guitar in Vietnam.

Nobody but me, that is.

DAY 297

On this day Delta Battery got temporarily split in half – the half I was assigned to was going on a mission to a place called Tra Bong five miles inland. We would coordinate with a battery of 175MM guns that were already there. Tra Bong was home to the *Montagnard* (a French word that we pronounced: 'mountain yard'), the indigenous peoples of the Central Vietnamese Highlands.

We choppered three guns with their crews and got there in the early afternoon and thought: 'now what?' There were no bunkers and no gun emplacements, just a football-sized plot of sandy soil in between a small river and a primitive village of crude, bronze-age huts.

The officer in charge instructed each of us to start digging a trench big enough for a cot. There was a stack of large, corrugated semi-culverts and we were going to use those as roofs for our trenches once our cots were fitted inside.

Our digging tool was the standard, folding Army *entrenching* tool – not a proper spade. Ugh. It was hard work but there was no choice about it.

My new hole, er, trench was about 150 feet from a 175MM howitzer and its crew which was already in place and shooting missions. This was the first 175 I'd ever seen in action and I thought my ears might never be the same – *loud* does not describe it. Our 105's were loud, the 175 seemed to be three-times louder.

As I'm digging I notice a weathered-looking Vietnamese guy has started plowing the field in between us and the village. It's like a photo out of an old National Geographic. He's strapped to a water buffalo as it pulls a crude, wooden plow about 200 feet from me. We were instructed to leave anything nonessential at LZ Buff, so I didn't bring my camera and don't have any photos.

A short time later, his wife (I presume) brought him some water. Nothing unusual about that except she's only wearing a ground-length skirt and sandals. Come to find out, tops are optional for Montagnard women when it's warm.

As the Banded Bay Cuckoo flies, we're only about 20 miles from Chu Lai but it's as if we've gone through some kind of time-warp portal. I'm wondering: how is it LIFE Magazine, National Geographic or Playboy never mentioned our G.I.'s encountering these primitive people with their topless women?

After my distraction returned to her village, I got back to the matter at hand: digging. Eventually, the trench is big and deep enough for my cot. I got help placing a couple culverts over it leaving enough clearance to crawl inside. Then, I filled a few sand bags to cover the culverts. My new home away from home away from home wasn't much, but it would have to do.

And if it wasn't for that damned 175MM gun firing every few hours, I would have gotten a pretty good night's sleep – I was hoping to dream about Montagnard women, but no such luck.

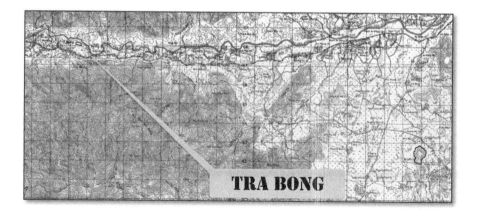

TRA BONG

DAY 301

Our mission at Tra Bong was never clear – it seemed like the powers that be were simply keeping us busy. A couple days after we got there, we folded our cots and returned to LZ Buff. The other half of Delta Battery didn't return – apparently, their mission hadn't been completed. So our contingent at Buff was at half strength.

I was, temporarily, the only guy in my bunker/hootch – the others were all part of the second half that hadn't returned.

It's another perfect day in Vietnam – crystal clear, deep blue skies and moderate temperatures in early May. I've just returned from lunch at the mess tent and was marveling at how nice and peaceful it was with half of us somewhere else when a black rat scurried towards me at full speed in the open, sandy area in front of my bunker.

Before I had the chance to think 'that was odd', a six-foot long, thick, black snake came into view close on the heels of the rat. Then, the rat made a hard right turn before he gets to me and . . .

PROCEEDS DOWN THE DIRT RAMP INTO MY BUNKER!
THE SNAKE FOLLOWS HIM!

I'm thinking 'HOLY SHIT!' as Corporal Dowdy wanders into view on my right. (continued on the next page)

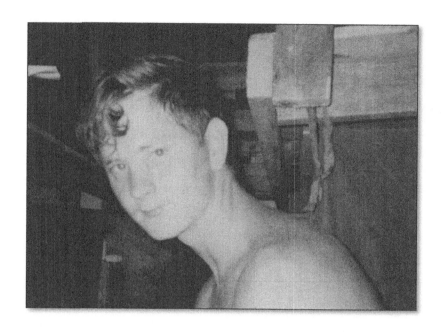

Sometimes I'm quick-witted and sometimes I wonder if there's something wrong with me, but on this occasion I instantly hatched a plan that would have made Tom Sawyer proud.

Corporal Dowdy was a gung-ho, young dude from Texas – only 18 or 19-years old. He had just been promoted to corporal. I don't like snakes – this was a job for a young Texan with something to prove.

Me: "Did you see that? A big snake just chased a rat into my hootch. Do you want to kill him?"

Dowdy: "You bet!"

Me: "What are you gonna use?"

Dowdy (finds an entrenching tool): "This!"

174

I let him lead the way down the ramp into the bunker – the only way in or out. As we headed in I told Dowdy:

"Let the snake catch the rat before you kill it."

Once inside we spotted the rat under my bunk. He was either saying his prayers or had gotten distracted by a crumb of food. The snake slithered up behind the rat, grabbed it with its mouth and wrapped its coils around the rodent in one continuous, rapid-fire movement as we watched.

A few minutes passed and the rat stopped moving. The snake's mouth opened tall and began ingesting it.

When it all was in, I looked at Dowdy, "NOW!"

Dowdy commenced chopping with extreme prejudice.

He cut the snake's head off and proudly carried the wriggling carcass out by the tail while I used the shovel to remove the head from my premises.

I'll bet Dowdy's told that tale at every bar he's ever visited since this day - not to mention to his kids and grandkids.

I was pretty pleased with myself, too. I conned him into doing it, but considering the heroic story he got out of the experience, I'd say we were even.

DAY 303 (NIGHT)

A little after midnight Delta Battery's First Sergeant paid me a most unexpected visit.

"Baskin! Wake up!"

I propped myself up on one arm. He had his M16 and as he ducked down in the short doorway there was just enough light for me to notice he was wearing his flak jacket and helmet.

Him: "We got an intel report there's VC in the area and we're gonna get hit. Get up and get ready. Better put your flak jacket and helmet on."

Me: "Yes, sir."

Him: "Guard this entrance. Shoot anyone who isn't one of us."

Me: "Yes, sir," and he left.

I had been sound asleep, but this snapped me out of it. His tone of voice told me this was not a drill. Something bad was about to happen – the terror we normally rained down on Charlie was about to visit us.

I followed his instructions – put on my flak jacket and helmet and positioned myself on the incline that was the entrance to my bunker.

The First Sergeant's last words communicated the expectation that our defensive perimeter could be penetrated - that I would need to defend myself against a foe determined to kill me.

A corporal I met back in Cherry Hill had told me about the night he was blind-sided on his base by a lone sapper. The G.I.'s name may have been Ed. The sapper knocked Ed down instead of shooting him. Ed's reflexes must have been pretty good 'cause he told me he swiveled his M16 up and fired a single round at point blank range. It sounded unusually heroic, but Ed was wearing an NVA belt with a bullet hole though the buckle's center.

The only thing that separated LZ Buff from Charlie was multiple coils of razor wire. We trained bright spotlights on every foot of that wire, but sometimes they were still able to get through it without our guards seeing them cutting their way in.

An illumination round shot into the sky as I chambered a round in the M16 and topped off the 20-round clip to insure I had 21 chances before reloading. I flipped the safety *off* and the 'mode' switch to *full auto*. If Charlie was going to try to kill me, I'd have an instant to get him first - I was determined to get off as many rounds as quickly as possible.

As I lay there in the dark my dad's farewell came to my mind: "Keep your head down, son. Don't be a hero."

Of course, he loved me and wanted me to return, but he knew I wasn't the fighter he was - that I was doing this to earn his respect and not because I was brave or felt duty bound. That small measure of complicity would have amplified his grief if worse came to worse and he encouraged me to play it safe.

Regardless, I was going to heed his advice and keep my head down – I wanted to live through this, too. I would defend my bunker and *engage* the enemy if he/they ran into my field of vision on the interior of our compound. I prayed that I saw him/them first.

Minutes ticked by with me lying there alone in the dark trying not to blink for fear I'd lose any advantage in an exchange with a sapper and hoping one of our guys didn't run past with me on this emotional knife edge - reminding myself not to shoot until I knew it wasn't one of us.

I've always been competitive and for me this was a contest – a life and death contest, to be sure, but a contest, nevertheless. If I had been put in this 'ring' with an adversary and one of us had to die, it wasn't going to be me.

My fear intensified with every passing moment. Mentally, I was prepared, even if I was a wreck emotionally.

There would be no hesitation on my part. If an enemy soldier came into my field of view in the center of our base, he's implicitly here to kill me or my comrades. I will hit him with as many rounds from my M16 as possible as soon as he comes into view.

In an instant, all hell broke loose on the perimeter of the base. It was as if the trigger to every gun, howitzer, mortar and quad 50 had been wired together and was pulled repeatedly. The fighting was far more intense than any firefight I ever saw recreated for movies or could have imagined.

I was simultaneously relieved that the waiting was over, thrilled by the incredible display of firepower and terrified a sapper would be in my vicinity at any moment.

Much of what I heard was Charlie's guns and Charlie's rockets hitting nearby targets on Buff. Rapid-fire explosions were visible everywhere. After one of the explosions, the distinctive sound of the quad 50 stopped.

I tried not to think about the guys I knew could be dying on our perimeter and focus on what was in front of me as the fighting continued.

An infantry mortar and one of our howitzers were alternately shooting illumination rounds, but they didn't always overlap. I could see the center of our compound in front of me while they were lit and it got very dark as soon as they burned out.

My sense of time was impaired, but after what seemed like a few minutes, the intensity of the fight started to diminish. Then it became sporadic and at about the 15 to 20 minute mark, it stopped though our illumination rounds continued.

As I crouched there I made a few assumptions: that the battle was over and that we had repelled Charlie. In hindsight it was a premature conclusion, but I decided it was time for me to get some company and I stuck my head out. It looked clear and I scrambled out of my bunker's entrance and sprinted to Delta Battery's command post about 30 feet away. There was no one guarding that entrance and I burst into the bunker.

I don't remember exactly what I said but I felt like I'd just won the latest round of 'Vietnam Roulette':
"Wow! That was something! We made it!"

The CO and First Sergeant gave me a look that told me they weren't ready to agree on behalf of the entire unit - they were still assessing the situation and damage. I think I was offered a cup of coffee and took a seat.

I asked if we had casualties and the First Sergeant told me a rocket had hit the quad 50 injuring the gunner, my guitar-playing friend Robert. They were getting reports from the 3 howitzer crews and the infantry across the way. At some point they figured they could sound the 'all clear'. The sarge told me I could go back to my bunker and get a few hours rest.

I can't believe I went back there alone – the illumination rounds had stopped and it wouldn't be light for at least 3 hours – the moon was a sliver that night and it was still dark as dark gets. Nevertheless, I went back and I think I actually went back to sleep!

DAY 303 (DAYLIGHT)

The scene and mood on LZ Buff were very different with this sunrise. The debris from last night's fight was just about everywhere – Charlie had showered us with RPG and mortar rounds whose tailfins were sticking out of sandbags on bunkers and in craters in the ground. The tailfin of one mortar was impaled 15 feet in front of the entrance to my bunker.

The bodies of dead VC sappers were being tossed on our ¾-ton truck for disposal and eight G.I. body bags lie near the mess tent.

Some of the dead VC had uniforms - some only had skimpy briefs. They weren't as bloody as I expected them to be and they were already stiff. One was missing his head and another an arm (probably) due the high velocity M16 rounds which tumble and saw through flesh when they hit bone. There were 27 in all.

(continued)

Those bodies stacked on the truck bed was I sight I'll never unsee. I considered taking photos, but thought better of it – even though they were enemies who had killed some of us and *would have killed all of us*, I felt that would have been wrong.

We drove them outside our perimeter, down to the LZ area where a small bulldozer was scraping a ditch for their burial. Two of us threw them into their resting place and the dozer finished up.

The Viet Cong force that attacked us last night was estimated at two companies. In 15-20 minutes, they bombarded LZ Buff with nearly 45 RPG rounds and 150 mortar rounds. Their sappers entered the compound under the cover of the barrage and overran a couple of the bunkers on the infantry side of our perimeter.

The mood on the hill was somber: no celebrations - no high fives - no back pats. *We* may have lived to fight another day, but eight didn't – eight of us were going home in body bags. Another twenty of us had been wounded and medivac-ed to Chu Lai.

All our dead were infantry except for one sergeant from the engineers. One of the dead infantry was their Captain John Yeatts.

In mid-afternoon, the 1/52nd held a tribute that ended with the traditional twenty-one gun salute honoring the fallen soldiers.

One of the survivors from 'A' Company, 1/52nd posted a severed VC head on our perimeter as a symbolic warning and a reminder to Charlie.

DAY 307

A few days after being overrun we had gotten back into our work routines on LZ Buff. This was another hot day of ammo humping for me – I needed a shower. It was close to sunset when I climbed the ladder, poured five gallons of water into the barrel above our open-air stall, removed my towel, lathered up and locked eyes with an attractive, American woman in a light blue outfit as she walked by.

Up to that point, the existence of the 'Donut Dollies' was a rumor I'd never confirmed. Her unfazed expression remained cheerful as she and her partner 'Dolly' continued towards the 1/52nd side of the hill. Apparently, the sight of a naked G.I. showering wasn't all that unusual.

Conversely, she was the first American woman I'd seen in over ten months. If there had been a memo regarding the Dollies' visit, I didn't get it. I was completely surprised and more than a little annoyed though outwardly my reaction wasn't different than hers. I earned that shower and this was *my turf*. If the sight of me was a problem, it wasn't *my* problem. I finished taking my shower.

As I've mentioned, there were zero American women in combat in Vietnam. On bases like Buff lacking access via roads, there weren't Vietnamese women, either. Consequently, privacy was not a consideration for toilets or showers or whatever. Our phone-booth-sized shower was doorless.

The 'Donut Dollies' were female, Red Cross volunteers who served in Vietnam. Their mission was to provide emotional support for us troops – a *touch of home* for the boys, a reminder of the girl next door, the sister and even the mother - cute, friendly and caring, not sexual, but there *had* to be guys who *tried* anyway. They traveled in pairs to fire support bases and brought with them games, snacks, soda, juice, *donuts* and most importantly, smiles.

They were specifically on Buff to perk up the infantry – those guys had lost their commander and twenty-seven of their buddies as a result of the recent attack.

I had a different take – I needed perking up as much as anybody, but I didn't want to be reminded of someone I couldn't be with by some surrogate/tease who would be forever gone a few minutes later.

Apparently, there were guys who felt like they benefitted from those visits, but I couldn't see how it would (benefit me) and (I) made no attempt to visit with them.

Regardless, those two Dollies must have now believed they knew why it was called LZ 'Buff'.

DAY 312

No sooner would the 'Dollie's' tale of the 'buff, showering G.I. at LZ Buff' have begun to circulate than somebody decided LZ Buff needed to be renamed.

Okay, maybe it was a coincidence, but our LZ was officially renamed 'LZ Stinson' today. Apparently, 'Stinson' was a high-ranking muckety-muck who died *somewhere else* in Vietnam two months ago.

How weird is that? If Buff needed a different/better name, why not honor 1/52nd C.O. Captain Yeatts who died fighting **here** a few days ago?

We continued to call it LZ Buff – partly out of habit and partly because the new name was so inappropriate.

DAY 319

Another day, another sweaty workout delivering a truckload of ammo to the guns. After Harold and I finished, I'm walking up to the entrance of my bunker/hootch and somebody hollers: "INCOMING!" I realize I'm supposed to duck, but I hesitated, looking around wondering who said that and how do they know there's 'incoming'?

Somebody else yells 'INCOMING' and I figured they weren't messing around. I broke into a run just as a mortar exploded on the nearest corner of the command bunker 30 feet from me – I saw the explosion as I ducked inside my bunker's doorway.

A gunner from one of Delta's Batteries who happened to be passing by was nicked by a piece of that mortar's shrapnel on his neck. He bled profusely.

He went straight into the command bunker and they patched him up. He was medivac-ed within an hour and we never saw him again.

I had been closer to the blast than that guy, but was untouched.

We received a few more rounds, but everyone had taken cover so, nobody else was injured as a result.

DAY 320

The G.I.'s who happened to see the *flashes* from yesterday's mortar rounds were able to pinpoint Charlie's location – he was just the other side of a ridge ¼ to ½ mile away from Buff. Under normal circumstances, our infantry might have been all over those VC the same day, but 1/52nd was still putting their pieces back together after the attack of May 12th. Furthermore, they weren't sure Charlie wasn't setting a trap – the handful of mortar rounds we received may have been bait intended to draw us into an ambush.

Our 105MM's were of no use – Charlie was too close.

So we slept with one eye open last night and scheduled an air strike for (this) morning. The fighter jet showed up just past noon – it put on quite a show and I grabbed my camera.

The fighter jet is (just) visible in the center of this photo.

The fighter jet just to the left of the plume in #2
and pulling out of its last run in #3.

189

After the jet had made a half dozen bombing and strafing runs on Charlie, the pilot circled around and gave us another thrill – he screamed *directly* over LZ Buff at treetop level traveling about 500 MPH. Wow!

There were no more stray mortar rounds hitting LZ Buff after that.

One of Delta Battery's new 105's in action.

DAY 324

LZ Buff had a small NCO club over on the 1/52nd side of the hill and after work I went there to pass some time. Some of the guys were throwing darts and I thought, "I'm pretty good throwing a baseball, maybe I'll give it a try."

It's kind of like shooting free throws in basketball or pitching in baseball, using the same muscles and motion over and over. Once you dial in the range, you can hit the target every time.

I beat the first guy I took on and another guy challenged me – he wanted to play for money. I agreed.

We started at $1. I won. He said, "Double or nothing." I agreed.

I won again. He repeated, "Double or nothing." I agreed again.

This went on until the tab was over $1000. The gang watching the contest was beside themselves at the prospect of a $1000 payoff, but I suspected I would never see the money.

He said, "Double or nothing."

I knew I should 'call' it, but I didn't.

I missed. He won. And I learned a lesson in gambling.

DAY 330

I've mentioned that there were zero women in combat and I've mentioned the volunteer 'Donut Dollies', but I haven't said anything about the women who served as nurses in Vietnam. That's primarily because I never met or saw or needed one – it wasn't part of my experience. Nevertheless, about 11,000 women did serve in our military hospitals all up and down the country throughout the war.

On this day (June 8th) the hospital in Chu Lai was attacked by rocket fire and a nurse was killed. She was Lieutenant Sharon Lane, the only American servicewoman killed by hostile fire in the Vietnam War.

On LZ Buff, we were about 10 miles away, but were never informed. I only found out about Lt. Lane's death many years later. A character in the 1980's TV series 'China Beach' was loosely based on Lt. Lane.

DAY 332

I debated with myself about mentioning this, but . . .

This is the day I discovered Marvel Comics and, specifically, 'THOR' as I was hanging out in one of the gun crews' bunkers.

I know in the context of *War* how trivial that sounds, but reading comic books was a typical pastime for our youthful G.I.'s in between combat missions.

I had never previously read a comic book that captured my interest – it was a mini 'AH-HA' moment. The only comics I'd ever encountered before were things like 'Archie' and its spinoffs, 'Jughead' and 'Betty and Veronica'. Ugh. Even 'Superman' was too artificial for me to embrace.

'Thor' was different - the plots of the stories were fresh, plausible (within the context of a comic book), a bit more intellectual and involved new villains. 'THOR' resonated with me and apparently, I wasn't the Lone Ranger where that's concerned.

I wonder what that says about the maturity of our troops in Vietnam? A comic book in one hand and an M16 or lanyard in the other...

DAY 343

By now I've hooked up dozens of loads to both Huey's and Chinooks, but I haven't completed the trifecta – I haven't hooked up The Flying Crane. The 'Crane' is Uncle Sam's biggest, ugliest, baddest chopper, but it's used sparingly on an 'as needed' basis and we hadn't as yet needed one.

Today, we're shipping a deuce and a half truck - the only chopper that can lift it is The Crane. Yep, I'm gonna get to cross that bad guy off my list.

I was expecting a bigger wash from its propellers as it approached, but not the hurricane force winds that nearly knocked me down. The down force of those blades was awesome!

When it was overhead, I clamored into the truck bed, stood still and held the noose high like always, but the crane's shape prevented it from descending to the normal level. It hovered a few feet higher as the hook was lowered by a motorized winch - that made the hook a free-swinging, 20-pound, steel pendulum. I had to adjust my technique on the fly and avoid getting clubbed by that thing.

It wasn't the first rodeo for the Crane's crew and they made me look like a pro as I lassoed the hook and dove for cover.

Trifecta complete, Sir!

DAY 351

It's always been my nature to see the cup as half full rather than half empty. So, I may be spending my days waiting for choppers to arrive, getting blasted by sand and pummeled by stones as they approach, risking my life when they hover just above my head and then sweating bullets in the 100° heat humping the ammo on and off the truck, but I considered the positive:

I'M GETTING THE BEST TAN OF MY LIFE and
I DON'T HAVE TWO OUNCES OF FAT ON MY ABS!

I know, it's not much consolation, but it'll have to do for another 14 days.

That is: ONLY FOR ANOTHER 14 DAYS! YAHOO!!

DAY 354

Another hot, sunny day. Captain Alexander had recently procured a small refrigerator for his personal use and stocked it with beer and Coke. I happened to be passing by his command bunker after distributing that day's ammo to the six guns and he asked if I'd like a cold beer or Coke. I don't remember if we were celebrating something or if he was making a 'job well-done' gesture or merely assuaging some guilt for the stupid-ass job he assigned me.

Would I ever! I hadn't acquired the taste for beer (yet), but I loved Coke. We had warm Cokes somewhat frequently, but *never* cold ones – a cold Coke was a huge treat.

At the time I was really thirsty and as he handed the can to me, I wondered how fast I would/could consume it. I popped it open and checked the second hand of my watch. When it got to the '12', I started gulping it down.

Four seconds flat.

Man, was it GOOD!

DAY 361

I GOT ORDERS TO GO HOME TODAY!

I'm scheduled to leave two days early by my count - the day after tomorrow. As they say: 'that's close enough for military work.'

WOO-HOO!

DAY 362

Tomorrow's the day I bid this awful place farewell ('good-bye' is too good a word) and today I've got one more thing to check off my 'Did-In-Vietnam' check list: 'fire my M16 on FULL AUTO'.

Maybe I'm lucky that it didn't get done before today, but if it was gonna get done, *today* had to be the day.

I've got another year and a half to go before my military obligation is completed and I don't know what I'll be doing, but I'm VERY SURE there will NEVER be an opportunity to fire an M16 on full auto in those eighteen months. An active combat zone is the ONLY place where the Army issues rifles the soldier maintains possession of and the ONLY place where someone could fire on 'full auto' as easily as walking to the edge of a firebase.

There were a few of us 'short-timers' in Delta Battery – the others were on various gun crews so I paid a visit to those crews and found three guys who were up for sharing in my little adventure.

I didn't know these guys very well but we were all on the same page. One of them had a gypsy bandana and one of them had a helmet that had been used for target practice that we passed around, acting out our disdain for the military and this miserable place. One of the guys had a portable turntable and stereo system that we brought with for added *ambiance*.

I was pretty sure we'd be able to shoot at will down by the LZ so we hiked down there. It was my idea so I shot first.

That got the attention of the nearest guard post and a soldier ran up to us to ask us what we were doing. He had a walkie-talkie and after we explained that we were going home and hadn't tested our M16's on full auto, he relayed the message to his *boss* who said: "Okay." The *boss* indicated a direction for us to fire that was free of any friendly personnel.

My turn – full auto! Hendrix playing on the portable turntable/stereo! Expended shells are all over the ground.

Once we had been cleared to shoot, we got down to some serious business. The four of us took turns so we could watch all the action. When it was my turn I held my finger on the trigger and emptied the 20-round clip *disappointingly* fast – 2 or 3 seconds. I started to reload, but we were attracting too much attention and the officer of the guard pulled the plug on our little *full-auto* party. Man, it was cool while it lasted.

DAY 363

This day is a blur. I don't remember much about leaving LZ Buff. I said my 'goodbyes' yesterday - my focus was getting off this hill and into Chu Lai to catch a flight for Saigon. I was more than eager to leave this nightmare behind.

I got a lift from a little 2-seater, Bell chopper en route to Chu Lai, but I don't remember the flight to Saigon (the latter would have been about two hours long). I do remember my anxiety – it wasn't over until I was out of Vietnam's air space.

My flight to the U.S. departed July 11th, 1969 from Tan Son Nhut Air Base. I boarded a World Airways flight, the same carrier used to ferry us G.I.'s to Vietnam. There were no empty seats and we were all in uniform. I had in a window seat on the right side of the plane. The flight was long and quiet – we were relaxed and there was zero rowdiness, zero celebrating.

That is, until the plane touched down at SeaTac Airport in Washington State – at that point we all breathed a huge, grateful sigh of relief and burst into an extended, cheering applause.

I had spent 363 days (almost 5% of my life) in Vietnam, I didn't know if I'd ever see the U.S. again and I was THRILLED to be back on American soil – we ALL were.

That emotion doubled for me when the door of the plane's cabin opened letting air in from the outside – I wasn't expecting it - it smelled like *home*. I'll never forget that moment and the feeling of security, normalcy and peace that accompanied it. Then, I *knew* I was home. It moves me to tears thinking about how powerful that feeling was.

It was over. I had made it back without a scratch, without psychological scars and without regrets.

I was one of the lucky ones.

DE-BRIEFING

This is where the author typically sums up, tries to make sense out of their narrative and produce a moral. If I (or anyone) could make sense out of the U.S. military mission to Vietnam, I'd/they'd have to be an expert spin-doctor - *sense* is something the Vietnam War lacked. If you watch Ken Burns' comprehensive documentary on Vietnam, after twenty hours you'll likely be scratching your head (like me) wondering: 'Why?'

In hindsight, it's crystal clear: we had NO business being there.

The moral? Don't send American troops to fight for a country unless that country is fully committed to helping themselves.

As far as my personal experiences are concerned, it kind of seems like the blind had been leading the blind. I, the figuratively blind G.I. was lead by blind or mostly impersonal leadership. There was little rhyme or reason to most of it. Yeah, I screwed up a few times, but after I demonstrated my aptitude, skill, dependability, adaptability and general agreeableness they still assigned me to a *grunt* job.

Looking back now, trying to understand my experience it appears as though I fell victim to an age-old military formula that was purely based on numbers of bodies: ours verses theirs.

Ultimately, it didn't matter what military occupation I had been trained for – as far as those in charge were concerned, I was a soldier who might have to plug whatever hole needed plugging.

Even so, I was one of the lucky ones who really *shouldn't* complain: unlike the 58,000 men who were killed, the 75,000 who were severely disabled and the 1200 who are *still unaccounted for*, I came home without a scratch. Additionally, I don't think I was exposed to 'agent orange' and I don't have PTSD flashbacks.

I have benefitted from that year of living dangerously in numerous ways. Uncle Sam helped finance the college education I completed after I got out and he under-wrote the mortgage of my first house.

Emotionally speaking, the confidence I earned by running that gauntlet of challenges gave me a **CAN DO** attitude in both personal and business decisions ever since.

I hope the tone of this journal hasn't created a false impression – the narrative could read like a marvelous *adventure* – it wasn't. Were it not for the danger, loneliness and absurdity of our mission . . . maybe - but those conditions permeated nearly every moment.

Would I do it again? Let me think for a second: NO. Writing this memoir had its good recollections, but dredged up as many bad ones. That's as close to reliving my tour of duty in Vietnam as I ever want to get.

Be that as it may . . .

. . . the experience was *priceless*.

"Missed it by that much."

TAPS

I met Roger McRight at church when I was seven. There were a number of young guys whose parents attended the little start-up Baptist church in Tinley Park, Illinois and we all became friends and grew up together. There was Randy Bauer, Darryl Melvin, Randy Curlee, Roger and me.

Roger's family and mine were kind of mirror images of each other. His Dad and my Dad became best friends; his Mom and my Mom became best friends and their family had three kids which were the same ages and genders as me, and my two sisters. Linda became friends with Susan, Carol became best friends with Robin and I became best friends with Roger. Those friendships lasted throughout each of our lives.

While growing up Roger and I played a lot of baseball and football together. We watched a lot of TV together - Rocky & Bullwinkle, Rin Tin Tin and The Mickey Mouse Club come to mind, but there were numerous other shows that we enjoyed. We went camping together. We played a lot of Davey Crockett, cowboys and indians and *soldiers* together. And we were in Sunday School giving the teacher a hard time together.

In our early teens.

As we got older some differences began to show up. I tended to be a bit serious and intellectual. Roger was rebellious and fun.

As teenagers we got interested in girls together though he was more successful at boy/girl relationships than me. Probably because he was more 'fun' and I was too serious.

We had lunch together every day at high school and hung out together in the hallways as much as possible.

It's only natural that we got in trouble together. One Sunday afternoon and we drove to the Michigan sand dunes together - 1.5 hours away - when we were supposed to be visiting a friend in Tinley Park. Then there were the vandalous escapades that will remain buried in the past. We went to jail together for one night.

We worked part time jobs together. It was Roger who got me on at a 'McDonalds-style' fast food restaurant in Harvey, Illinois. Then I returned the favor by getting him on at Ed & Joe's Pizza in Tinley Park as a delivery man/short order cook.

Roger was filling in for me one night after I sliced my thumb on the meat slicer. I kept him company on a pizza delivery when he hit a child with his car – it was unavoidable and I would have been driving was it not for the slicer accident.

The little boy ran across the road in the middle of town right in front of him. Coincidentally, it was at the location where he and I had met - the Baptist Church building now housed the Jehovah's Witnesses whose Wednesday service had just ended.

Roger was scared and tempted to drive away, but I convinced him to stop. The child's parents saw exactly what happened and realized that Roger was not at fault and didn't press charges. Miraculously, the child was somehow not seriously injured.

After high school I went to college while Roger finished high school and attended a technical school in Alabama to learn helicopter maintenance. I wasn't cut out for advanced calculus and after an unsuccessful two years at the University of Illinois in Chicago, I enlisted in the Army.

My last conversation with Roger was via telephone after I had gotten back from Vietnam. I was stationed in Virginia at the time. Roger had enlisted in the Army with two local friends on the 'buddy' program. The deal was they would go through their military experience together.

It turned out to be a poor choice.

One of those buddies had failed some component of the military requirement and never served in Vietnam. The other buddy only qualified to be an infantryman - Roger's expertise at maintaining helicopters - a vital means of transportation in Vietnam - would never be utilized because his buddy didn't have that training and the Army's common denominator was: 'infantryman'.

(continued)

At lunchtime in December of 1969 I was in my barracks, having a year remaining of my military duty when I got a letter from my Dad. It started: "Son, this is the hardest letter I've ever had to write . . . "

A sniper's bullet had ended Roger's life.

I felt like it had ended a large part of mine, too. I burst into tears and lay on my bunk sobbing for several minutes. The thirty or so other guys respected my grief by leaving the room.

Roger hadn't been in Vietnam very long. He was on patrol with his platoon, walking the 'point'. Just like Roger: 'what me worry? Sure, I'll take the point . . . '

His buddy Tim was there when Roger was killed. I can't imagine how terrible Tim felt or feels today.

I thought I had put his loss behind me, but as I'm writing this 50 years later, my eyes are welling up.

I miss my friend and honor his valor and sacrifice.

Roger Lynn McRight

Every day should be 'Memorial Day' for those who
paid the price of our freedom with their lives.

'363 Days In Vietnam' is M.S.Baskin's 4th book. His diverse passions have yielded a variety of genres. To date, he's written an epic, mythological, graphic novel ('The Living Water'), a comprehensive investigation comparing religions ('Nine DeVine Theses') and a novice's guide to classical music ('Born to Write Music'). All books on Amazon.

The untold epic of Lilith, Adam's mythical first wife. Her amazing journey begins as she is banished from Eden. A guardian angel escorts her to the nearest city, Uruk, whose King Enmerkar is captivated by her beauty and makes her his queen. However, she falls in love with her angel and seeks the magical water of Eden in order to spend eternity with him. The demon Eblis tracks her out of Eden and initiates a plan to use her to get the water for himself. He tricks Lilith into helping him invade Eden to get it. The fate of the world hangs in the balance over the battle to possess The Living Water. Available in paperback, ebook and deluxe hardbound editions (by special order from the author: audioclassic@earthlink.net)

Does God exist? If so, which one?
It's the $64 trillion dollar question. Everybody has a belief about it one way or another. Among those who favor His existence there is an impressive diversity of opinion – are any of the contemporary religions true? Nine conclusions form the foundation of this theology. These conclusions or 'theses' are organized in a specific order – Volume One covers the first five. The name 'Nine DeVine Theses' is a play on words related to Luther's '95 Theses'. A word of caution: These 'nine theses' will challenge some or all of your beliefs. Available in paperback and ebook editions.

While every musical genre is a distinct dialect within the universal language of music, the 'classical' dialect is undoubtedly the most complex and hardest to appreciate. There are symphonies, concertos, tone poems, contatas, oratorios, operas, overtures, sonatas in the styles of the Renaissance, Baroque, Classical, Romantic, Impressionist and Modern Eras not including mixtures and neo versions. It's a LOT to comprehend. B2WM is for the novice wondering where to start their pursuit of the classical genre - a quick reference of the world's best composers with convenient access to their compositions. Available in ebook only.

THE AUTHOR

Michael Stuart Baskin

Made in the USA
Monee, IL
16 February 2023

27990839R00118